Michel Luc

Bellemare

INSURRECTION/POSTMODERNISM

Blacksatin Publications Inc.

2018

Blacksatin Publications Ltd.

[ISBN: 978-09781151-6-6]

CONTENT

PART TWO:

"Above the bodily man, there does not exist something higher. No thought is sacred…no feeling is sacred…no belief is sacred. They are all…[spooks]…created by…us. [They] exist only as… bogie(s) and phantasm(s) in [the] brain."

(Max Stirner, The Ego And His Own.)

"The essence of oligarchical rule is… the persistence of a certain world-view and a certain way of life. Who wields power is not important, provided that the hierarchical structure [and meta-narrative] remains always the same."

(George Orwell, 1984.)

Introduction:

Insurrection/Postmodernism is a call to arms, both conceptual and material, for everyone, who is truly sick and tired of inequality, tyranny, and bourgeois-capitalist mediocrity, at every level of socio-economic existence. In fact, *Insurrection/Postmodernism* is a series of essays, unmasking the meta-narrative of bourgeois-capitalism for what it is, another Enlightenment grand-narrative, regulating, controlling, and dominating, the plurality of micro-narratives, which circulate, create, and interrelate, the incommensurable island-narratives, in and across, the micro-recesses of our everyday lives. The point is to expose the meta-narrative of bourgeois-capitalism for what it is, totalitarianism, namely, a lie and a fallacy, perpetrated upon the general-population in the name of bourgeois-capitalism, so as to cunningly accumulate money and power in the hands of a select few, the state-finance-corporate-aristocracy. The point of *Insurrection/Postmodernism* is to show that the meta-narrative of bourgeois-capitalism is a form of totalitarianism, imposed upon the general-population, bent on destroying and eliminating differences, equality and autonomy, from the sum of socio-economic existence in favor of bourgeois unity, bourgeois-money and a despotic, bourgeois-capitalist totality.

The truth of the matter is that when the meta-narrative of bourgeois-capitalism grinds to a halt and/or collapses, and there are signs all-over that it inevitably will, a lot of incompetent people, who were wrongfully elevated into the upper-echelons of the bourgeois-capitalist-system, due to their obedience, ignorance, subservience, and overwhelming mediocrity, pertaining to the meta-narrative of bourgeois-capitalism, will be first against the wall, not for their crimes against humanity, per se, but, due to their docile ineptitude, stupidity, and total lack of empathy, which has resulted in endless socio-economic sufferings in and across everyday life. As a result, a large number of technocratic degenerates, who blindly follow, worship, and enact, the dictates of the meta-narrative of bourgeois-capitalism, without thinking, or empathy, with certain glib and religious fanaticism, will eventually face the full, unbridled, onslaught of pragmatic demolitionism, both mentally and physically etc., without remorse. It is no longer a matter of justice. We are well pass that. This concerns nothing less than pure and absolute retribution. Postmodernism commands and demands satisfaction, including its full maturation and apex. No longer is it content to remain stunted, arrested and castrated, muted and flattened, beneath the celebratory degenerate monologue, that is, the meta-narrative of bourgeois-capitalism. As a result, postmodernism insists upon insurrection and demolition. It insists on reaching and attaining the Nth degree of equality, autonomy, and heterogeneity, i.e., anarchism, whereupon, the maxim "anything goes" can be fully implemented to determine the sum of politics and global economics. Radical equality for all, but, first and foremost, economic financial equality, for all.

It is important to note that radical postmodernism, fully-developed postmodernism, is synonymous with anarchism, that is, inclusivity, heterogeneity, autonomy, equality and pragmatic-egalitarianism. It is only a stunted, castrated, postmodernism, which is identified with the ravages of bourgeois-state-capitalism. Given the chance to fully-blossom, postmodernism shall reveal the full-maturation of its raison d'être, structural-anarchism, due to the fact that the essence of postmodernism and anarchism are the same, pragmatic-egalitarianism, a plural-collectivity of micro-narratives, sharing all resources, in relative equal measure, within an open-participatory-democracy.

The meta-narrative of bourgeois-capitalism is all that stands in the way of anarchist postmodernism, that is, in the way of its full maturation and apex. The Enlightenment meta-narrative of bourgeois-capitalism is the only lynch-pin left, the last standing beach-head of the Enlightenment, the last standing iron-curtain, preventing, the full realization of full-blown anarchist postmodernism, devoid of unity, totality and any overarching universal criterion, meant to impede the advent of radical social change and open-participatory-democracy.

Of course, the meta-narrative of bourgeois-capitalism is both a singular totality and a litany of small partialities, i.e., a set of variable standpoints, reflecting variations, or interpretations, of the overall meta-narrative of bourgeois-capitalism. Different spheres of production, consumption, and distribution, despite, conforming to the parameters set by the meta-narrative of bourgeois-capitalism, function and operate, differently, depending on the parameters of their specific capitalist spheres and logical arrangements.

Notwithstanding, despite these variations in standpoint and interpretation, any capitalist sphere of production, consumption, and distribution, whatever it may be, if subjugated under the dominion of the meta-narrative of bourgeois-capitalism, must adhere to a singular, underlying logic, i.e., the logic of capitalism. That is, the capitalist logic which demands and commands the maximization of capitalist profit, by any means necessary, at lowest financial cost, as soon as possible.

Subsequently, it does not matter how, who, when, where and/or what, executes the dictates of the logic of capitalism, the point is that the logic of capitalism must reach maximum optimization, as soon as possible. As a result, the meta-narrative of bourgeois-capitalism is, in effect, comprised of a litany of in-commensurable and/or radically different socio-economic models, all of which, despite their differences in extracting and accumulating capital and profit, nonetheless, adhere to the logic of capitalism and the imperative of optimum capitalist performance. Therefore, despite their seemingly radical, socio-economic differences in and across bourgeois-state-capitalism, which are only superficial differences, the unifying thread weaving all these capitalist variabilities, into a cohesive whole, is the logic of capitalism. Namely, the logic of capitalism that is forever commanding, maximum profit and maximum efficiency, by any means necessary, as soon as possible.

At the moment, post-modernism, by itself, is an incomplete project, due to the fact that it does not go far enough. It has not fully comprehended its inherent motor force, anarchism. Therefore, it has not yet smashed to pieces the last remaining grand-narrative of the Enlightenment, i.e., bourgeois-capitalism. Anarchism is the material force of post-modernism and post-modernism is conceptual force of anarchism. Divorced from anarchism, post-modernism and its campaign for the maximization of plurality, autonomy, and egalitarianism, devoid of all grand-narratives, has not come to pass. Therefore, post-modernism has not fully realized itself, namely, it has not fully-bloomed, reached it apex, and presented its structural outputs in all their splendors. For this, it requires the brunt force of anarchism.

In consequence, the hand full of old postmodernists, who have described the coming of the post-modern age have only done so partially, due to the fact that their forms of post-modernism continue to admix with the vestiges of the Enlightenment, currently, embodied in the only grand-narrative of the Enlightenment, which truly matters, i.e., bourgeois-capitalism. The fact is the meta-narrative of bourgeois-capitalism has yet to succumb to the radical, anti-Enlightenment criticism level against it by the old postmodernists. The reason is that post-modernism has not fully come to terms with its motor force, anarchism, anarchism being the post-modern critique actualized in material-form on the ground. As a result, post-modernism has remained atrophied, stunted, and partially, undeveloped, a servant of bourgeois-capitalism. So, like an outdated, out-of-touch, old man/woman, who utterly refuses to retire, or give up his or her position to the new generation, the meta-narrative of bourgeois-capitalism, clings to its supremacy, with a certain totalitarian fanaticism, never been seen before, utterly oblivious to its senility, incompetence and obsolescence.

To such a radical extent does bourgeois-capitalism cling to power, that now, it in fact impedes any progress, any deviation and/ or any development, which it does not directly approve of and/or which does not directly improve its current station at the center of everyday life and socio-economic existence. The meta-narrative of bourgeois-capitalism is a sickness unto death, it is a rabid conservative fascism, functioning and operating, in and across socio-economic existence, asphyxiating, the novel, the creative, and the innovative, in the name of capitalist profit and a lame bourgeois-capitalist status quo. As a result, the meta-narrative of bourgeois-capitalism has condemned all forms of post-modernism, which have not jettisoned the inherent motor force of anarchism to the dust-bin of history.

Crushed beneath the lumbering meta-narrative of bourgeois-capitalism, these innocuous types of post-modernism, devoid of anarchism, become alibis and apologies for the tyranny of bourgeois-capitalism. It is post-modernism de-fanged! It is post-modernism domesticated,tamed, and slyly turned into a lame bourgeois plaything and pastime. Yet, the time is soon coming, and it will, wherefore, the workforce and the general-population, will have no recourse other than to blast the sum of bourgeois-capitalism to smithereens, including all degenerate forms of docile, senile, bourgeois post-modernism. Essentially, bourgeois-law, bourgeois-politics, bourgeois-education and the bourgeois-university etc., will all see blood-red in the narrow-minded streets of their despotic miniature dictatorships. And, nothing shall remain unscathed as the time has come to do away completely, with the meta-narrative of bourgeois-capitalism, so as to make way for the future, radical post-modernity, namely, undiluted demolitionism, that is, anarchist postmodernism.

So, at the opportune instant, embrace the disintegration and demolition of the meta-narrative of bourgeois-capitalism. Do not flinch! Throw your brick for liberty! And, throw it for equality! Throw your brick for democracy! And, throw it for anarchy! As, this is a bomb, nicely packed in a brown paper bag, left outside the revolving-doors of the bourgeois-capitalist edifice, eloquently exposing that this so-called grand-narrative is but another absolute metaphysical nothing, ready to die.

"Anarchism, Now! Anarchism, Forever! Anarchism, The Future!"

PART ONE

Ch.1:

Anarchism & Post-Modernism

Anarchism is the engine of post-modernism and post-modernism is the spirit of anarchism in the sense that both are the zenith and apex of radical social change, radical plurality, radical equality, and pragmatic-egalitarianism in its purest form. According to Errico Malatesta, anarchism "in common with socialism, has as its basis [and] point of departure… equality"[1], just as post-modernism "is a social universe… formed by…plurality…[whereupon] all things [are in essence] equal"[2]. For Jean-Francois Lyotard, post-modernism "is an attitude that [is]…libertine or libertarian"[3], meaning, it is a form of anarchism, a form of thought that is anarchistic in nature. Consequently, anarchism and post-modernism are synonymous. Anarchism and post-modernism are synonymous in the sense that post-modernism is epistemological anarchism in thought-form, i.e., narrative-form, and anarchism is pragmatic post-modernism in active-form, i.e., methodological-form. Specifically, anarchism is post-modernism operating on the ground, working in and across the micro-recesses of everyday life, physically attempting to demolish the totalitarian unity of bourgeois-capitalism into a post-modern, socio-economic plurality. Likewise, post-modernism is anarchism operating in theory, working in and across the micro-recesses of everyday life, mentally attempting to demolish the totalitarian unity of bourgeois-capitalism into an anarchist, socio-economic plurality. In short, anarchism and post-modernism are synonymous in the sense that they have similar foundations, namely, radical equality, radical plurality and a radical antipathy towards meta-narratives, including the meta-narrative of bourgeois-capitalism.

First and foremost, anarchism is pragmatic demolition, that is, the post-modern critique actualized in material-form, while, post-modernism is theoretical demolition, that is, the anarchist critique actualized in conceptual-form, both champion plurality, heterogeneity, and egalitarianism among all narratives. Anarchism is the methodology of post-modernism and post-modernism is the epistemology of anarchism, hence, why both are synonymous with each other, i.e., two sides of the same coin, two peas in the same pod, wherein, the goal for both is to "maximize as much as possible the multiplication of small narratives... [whereupon] none is privileged"[4].

For both, anarchism and post-modernism, "all... positions are equivalent"[5], which should equitably translate into what Proudhon refers to as "the necessary condition [for an] equality of fortunes"[6]. For, both anarchism and post-modernism, an equality of positions means every narrative should be on an equal plain, wherefore, none is more privileged than another. Simultaneously, for anarchism and post-modernism, an equality of positions means as well an equality of fortunes, wherefore, no-one is legitimately more privileged than another in possessing a greater fortune than his or her neighbour. As Proudhon states, "society necessarily [implies] equality"[7], while, "property is the negation of equality"[8], that is, "property is anti-social"[9]. Property negates society. In effect, for Proudhon, "property and society are utterly irreconcilable"[10]. Ultimately, meaning, there is no legitimate basis for any inequality of fortune and property in the sense that all positions are equivalent and inherently equal in status, which undermines any notion of legitimacy, pertaining to the unequal distribution of property and wealth.

In effect, the principle of equality underlying anarchism and post-modernism, reveals that all inequalities of property and fortune are illegitimate, unfounded and, in fact, impede socio-economic development. As Proudhon states, "the principle of equality kills…the principle of property"[11], and "when property is widely distributed [via equality], society thrives [and]…when property is concentrated [via inequality], society abuses itself"[12].

It is for this reason that Proudhon argues "property originates in violence"[13]. For it cannot exist "without robbery and murder"[14], due to the fact that property and fortune contradict the inherent principle of equality underlying life and socio-economic existence. Society suffers when property thrives too much. Consequently, there is no legitimate reason and/or logic for the existence of bourgeois-capitalism other than force, coercive force, since, bourgeois-capitalism is all about the illegitimate confiscation of property. As Proudhon articulates, "property rests first on war and conquest, then on treatise and agreements"[15]. And, since, there is no real legitimate reason for the inequality of property and fortune other than violence and force, treatise and agreements serve only to legalize inequality, fortunes and robbery, which is exactly what anarchism and post-modernism have always implied with their radical critiques and notion of radical equality. Power decides not verity, when, according to Lyotard, "all opinions are acceptable"[16].

Notwithstanding, for both anarchism and post-modernism, decision-making-authority and the distribution of power should be guided by the maximization of plurality. According to Lyotard, what

> we need today in order to make decisions cannot be the idea of totality, or of unity,…it can only be the

> idea of a multiplicity or a diversity. [Namely, to] always act in such a way that the maxim of your will may…not be erected…into a principle of universal legislation…[but] into a principle of… multiplicity. [17]

For Lyotard, it must be plurality that guides decision-making-authority and the distribution of resources in the sense that it must be the maxim of plurality, which tries to maximizes the greatest amount of plurality for all, instead of any notion of despotic totality and/or unity. Ultimately, for post-modernism and anarchism, in the last analysis, equality rules. The principle of equality trumps all values in the end. Only equality is legitimate. And, the more things are equalized among people and narratives, the more valid a form of distribution becomes.

In similar fashion, according to anarchist, Errico Malastesta, pluralism is the guiding principle of decision-making-authority and distribution of resources in the sense that

> there is [no] one solution to…social problems, but a thousand different and changing solutions in the same way as social existence is different and varied [both] in time and space…Unanimity of thought and identical conditions are impossible [and]. . . in my opinion, undesirable. [18]

For Malastesta, unanimity of thought is undesirable because it tyrannizes over the necessities of plurality and equality. For him, the necessary principles for any decision-making-authority are equality and plurality, only equality and plurality can give rise to "a network of needs and ideas which reciprocally give rise to and re-enforce one another"[19]. The point, for Malastesta, is the creation of a plural "intelligent decentralization"[20], wherefore, in effect, according to Lyotard, "a multiplicity of small narratives"[21] is manifested, devoid of any overarching meta-narrative, specifically, the meta-narrative of bourgeois-capitalism. The concepts of radical equality and radical plurality lie at the core of both anarchism and post-modernism as both are attempts to dissolve all forms of totalitarianism, both conceptual totalitarianism and material totalitarianism. The objective, for both post-modernism and anarchism, is the creation of a socio-economic plurality, a plurality of micro-narratives embodying multiple nodes of power and decision-making-authority.

Likewise, for anarchist, Mikhail Bakunin, the objective of anarchism is to "create…[a] diversity of ideas, interests and aspirations"[22]. The point of any form of anarchism is to create and "to embrace [an] infinite multiplicity and diversity of interests…[and] of needs"[23], within the loose parameters of a post-capitalist, anarchist socio-economic formation. The same objective applies for post-modernism. Similar to Lyotard and his notion that "there is no reference [, or norms,] by which to judge"[24], Bakunin, in an identical line of thought argues:

> It is impossible to determine a concrete, universal… norm. The life of each…is subordinated to a plethora of different historical, geographical, and economic conditions, making it impossible to establish a model of organization [, both conceptual and/or material,] equally valid for all. Any such attempt would be absolutely impractical. It would smother the richness of… life which flourishes only in infinite diversity. [25]

In many ways, anarchism and post-modernism are fighting for the same ends as they fight against the implementation of a unitary world-view, i.e., meta-narrative. The goal for both anarchism and post-modernism is to prevent the implementation of a unitary meta-narrative onto existence. That is, any meta-narrative that invariably eliminates or seriously curtails pluralist freedoms, by confining natural heterogeneity into a specific, highly-condensed, artificial meta-narrative and/or world-view, namely, a meta-narrative and world-view, which denies the natural plurality of human existence, the fount of all freedoms. According to Michel Foucault, a world-view or meta-narrative, does nothing but "impose…the same norms and a certain structure of thought [upon society] that …men [and women]…cannot escape"[26], which, in the end, negate, according to Bakunin, "diversity…and those differences [that]…constitute…the abundance of humanity"[27].

In fact, this is what anarchism and post-modernism are, simultaneously, attempting to override and overcome, conceptually and materially, namely, the tyranny of any singular, overarching meta-narrative, which imposes an ironclad unified set of "homogeneous…regularitics…[upon humanity, i.e., a totalizing] discursive formation"[28] that governs the workings of micro-narratives, circulating in and across the stratums of everyday life. The point, the micro-narratives of anarchism and post-modernism are trying to make is that, through plurality and greater pragmatic-egalitarianism, inequality for all can be minimized, while, freedom for all, in contrast, can be maximized in the sense that the "freedom of each is…realizable only in the equality of all" [29]. For Bakunin, "freedom and equality are impossible without social and economic equality"[30] and the only way to achieve this is through the demolition of all meta-narratives, specifically, the meta-narrative of bourgeois-capitalism.

Like the radical antipathy that post-modernism expresses conceptually for meta-narratives, anarchism expresses a radical antipathy materially for meta-narratives. For both post-modernism and anarchism, bourgeois-capitalist "authority is the negation of freedom" [31] and, as a result, this demands an unyielding incredulity towards meta-authority. It demands constant demonstrations that "there is no [overarching] ontology"[32], i.e., intrinsic principle, which can justify meta-authority and/or meta-narrative. For anarchism and post-modernism, "equality and…freedom…[are] incompatible with any and all [meta-narratives]" [33], including the meta-narrative of bourgeois-capitalism. Both anarchism and post-modernism, demand a freedom capable of

> destroying all the dogmatic, metaphysical, political, and juridical fetters by which everyone today is loaded down, which will give everybody, collective as well as individual, full autonomy in their [narrative] activities and their [material] development, delivering one and...all from [the meta-narrative of bourgeois-capitalism]. [34]

For both anarchism and post-modernism, "the passion for destruction is a creative passion, too" [35] in the sense that it liberates equality and plurality from the despotic clutches of tyranny, the tyranny of meta-narratives. And, this destructive passion stems from the fact that there is no overarching ontology by which to determine any universal truth and/or judgment by. As Lyotard states, "there is no place from which one [can understand] the whole"[36] in the sense that "we are always within opinion"[37] because there is no real ontology, or ground, upon which to fasten any universal truth and/or judgment upon. Therefore, no meta-narrative, whatsoever, is valid or capable of being a justified, all-encompassing totality. A meta-narrative always imposes its rule onto another with certain coercive force, whether, this is soft or obdurate.

Subsequently, like anarchism, post-modernism argues that nothing is, in reality, legitimately privileged over another in the sense that like anarchism, post-modernism ascribes to Bakunin's notion that "the freedom of other[s]….far from negating or limiting my freedom, is, on the contrary its necessary condition and confirmation"[38]. The freedom of other micro-narratives, i.e., the limits of their freedom, expresses and reflects the freedom of one's own micro-narrative, i.e., the limits of one's own freedom. And, when a meta-narrative encroaches on the freedom of another micro-narrative, it simultaneously encroaches on the freedom of all micro-narratives.

As Bakunin states, "the oppression of one is the oppression of all, and we cannot violate the liberty of one… without violating the freedom of all" [39]. And, in similar anarchist fashion, Lyotard states "who [or what] is right? It is up to everyone to decide" [40]. It is not a matter of a select few imposing their will on the masses, which can only be unjust, but, it is the masses who must decide for themselves what is right. Meaning, it is the sum of all micro-narratives, together, which must decide, not the myopic views of a meta-narrative. And, according to Lyotard, "what will be [deemed] just ultimately is that upon which people agree... is just" [41]. That is, "it is [only] the common opinion"[42] of all micro-narratives, which can determine what equitable justice is and should be. Similarly, Bakunin states, "the only kind of justice that may have authority amongst us…can only be won by and founded upon the solidarity of [all] people [living] in [full] liberty"[43]. Any cabal, or class, living high above, imposing a meta-narrative on the general-population, is illegitimate and anti-social. It is a violation of freedom and a violation of the concept of plurality. It is fundamentally the negation of equality and, in general, the concept of society.

All in all, it is in this regard that anarchism and post-modernism are synonymous in the sense that both is founded upon and attempts to maximize, liberty, equality, justice and plurality for all micro-narratives, in relative equal measure, while, demonstrating the invalidity and illegitimacy of any overarching meta-narrative and/or world-view. Both argue that meta-narratives oppress and impose their will on the masses, denying them, the full expression of plurality, liberty, equality and justice for all. Both anarchism and post-modernism comprehend and argue that freedom and equality are fundamentally linked and based, first and foremost, upon socio-economic equality in the sense that economic "equality [is] the indispensable precondition for all freedoms"[44]. To deny socio-economic equality to the greatest number is, simultaneously, to deny the greatest number their fundamental right to the means of life and the full expression of their freedoms. Thus, the reason why the meta-narrative of bourgeois-capitalism impedes human development through private property, money and the profit-imperative.

Notwithstanding, while the micro-narrative of post-modernism focuses its attention and demolitionist critique upon the conceptual tyrannies of meta-narratives, i.e., the meta-narrative of bourgeois-capitalism, anarchism focuses its attention and demolitionist critique upon the material tyrannies of meta-narratives, i.e., the institutions of bourgeois-capitalism. The objective for both anarchism and post-modernism is to marshal, together, "the mother of all liberty, [namely], the tradition of revolt, …the realization of…[absolute] freedom,"[45] as "freedom can be created only by freedom, by a total rebellion of people"[46]. That is, a rebellion capable of completely and utterly demolishing the Enlightenment meta-narrative of bourgeois-capitalism so as to allow the full-maturity of post-modernity and anarchism to take place, through the egalitarian concepts of radical equality and plurality.

Ultimately, the apex and the zenith of post-modernism and anarchism is to be achieved via "the free organization of [micro-narratives] from the bottom up" [47], devoid of any federal state-apparatus and any overarching, governing meta-narrative. The goal is a conceptual and material people's revolution, capable of overturning the Enlightenment meta-narrative of bourgeois-capitalism, while, simultaneously, installing an anarchist federation/patchwork of micro-narratives, whereupon, no narrative is privileged over any other. And, each shares, in relative equal measure, the sum of all socio-economic resources in and across the newly-installed, post-modern, post-capitalist, anarchist society.

All in all, both post-modernism and anarchism represent radical equality, radical plurality and a radical antipathy towards all meta-narratives. And, both post-modernism and anarchism strive for the revolutionary implementation of radical egalitarianism in and across the sum of everyday life via conceptual and physical acts of pragmatic demolitionism.

Endnotes:

[1] Errico Malatesta, *The Method of Freedom*, ed. David Turcato, (Edinburgh, Scotland: AK Press, 2014) p. 3.
[2] Jean-Francois Lyotard and Jean-Loup Thebaud, *Just Gaming*, Trans.Wlad Godzich, (Minneapolis: University of Minnesota Press, 1985) p. 58.
[3] Ibid, p. 62.
[4] Ibid, pp. 59-60.
[5] Ibid, p. 74.
[6] Joseph Proudhon, *What Is Property?*, (United-States: Loki's Publishing, 2017) p. 75.
[7] Ibid, p. 136.
[8] Ibid, p. 128.
[9] Ibid, p. 31.
[10] Ibid, p. 31.
[11] Ibid, p. 40.
[12] Ibid, p. 197.
[13] Ibid, p. 98.
[14] Ibid, p. 107.
[15] Ibid, p. 33.
[16] Jean-Francois Lyotard and Jean-Loup Thebaud, *Just Gaming*, Trans. Wlad Godzich, (Minneapolis: University of Minnesota Press, 1985) p. 81.
[17] Ibid, p. 94.
[18] Errico Malatesta, *Errico Malatesta: His Life and Ideas*, ed. Vernon Richards, (London: Freedom Press, 1984) pp. 151-152.
[19] Errico Malatesta, *The Method of Freedom*, ed. David Turcato, (Edinburgh, Scotland: AK Press, 2014) p. 155.
[20] Errico Malatesta, *Errico Malatesta: His Life and Ideas*, ed. Vernon Richards, (London: Freedom Press, 1984) p. 25.

[21] Jean-Francois Lyotard and Jean-Loup Thebaud, *Just Gaming*, Trans. Wlad Godzich, (Minneapolis: University of Minnesota Press, 1985) p. 59.

[22] Mikhail Bakunin, *Bakunin On Anarchy*, ed. Sam Dolgoff, (New York: Vintage Books, 1972) p. 205.

[23] Ibid, p. 268.

[24] Jean-Francois Lyotard and Jean-Loup Thebaud, *Just Gaming*, Trans. Wlad Godzich, (Minneapolis: University of Minnesota Press, 1985) p. 43.

[25] Mikhail Bakunin, *Bakunin On Anarchy*, ed. Sam Dolgoff, (New York: Vintage Books, 1972) p. 77.

[26] Michel Foucault, *The Archeology of Knowledge*, trans. A.M. Sheridan-Smith, (New York, New York: Routledge, 1972) p. 191.

[27] Mikhail Bakunin, *Bakunin On Anarchy*, ed. Sam Dolgoff, (New York: Vintage Books, 1972) p. 88.

[28] Michel Foucault, *The Archeology of Knowledge*, trans. A.M. Sheridan-Smith, (New York, New York: Routledge, 1972) p. 145.

[29] Mikhail Bakunin, *Bakunin On Anarchy*, ed. Sam Dolgoff, (New York: Vintage Books, 1972) p. 76.

[30] Ibid, p. 99.

[31] Ibid, p. 238.

[32] Jean-Francois Lyotard and Jean-Loup Thebaud, *Just Gaming*, Trans. Wlad Godzich, (Minneapolis: University of Minnesota Press, 1985) p. 65.

[33] Mikhail Bakunin, *Bakunin On Anarchy*, ed. Sam Dolgoff, (New York: Vintage Books, 1972) p. 305.

[34] Ibid, p. 284.

[35] Ibid, p. 55.

[36] Jean-Francois Lyotard and Jean-Loup Thebaud, *Just Gaming*, Trans. Wlad Godzich, (Minneapolis: University of Minnesota Press, 1985) p. 43.

[37] Ibid, p. 43.

[38] Mikhail Bakunin, *Bakunin On Anarchy*, ed. Sam Dolgoff, (New York: Vintage Books, 1972) p. 5.

[39] Ibid, p. 68.

[40] Jean-Francois Lyotard and Jean-Loup Thebaud, *Just Gaming*, Trans. Wlad Godzich, (Minneapolis: University of Minnesota Press, 1985) p. 68.

[41] Ibid, p. 76.

[42] Ibid, p. 76.

[43] Mikhail Bakunin, *Bakunin On Anarchy*, ed. Sam Dolgoff, (New York: Vintage Books, 1972) p. 105.

[44] Ibid, p. 179.

[45] Ibid, p. 305.

[46] Ibid, p. 332.

[47] Ibid, p. 331.

Ch.2:

From Deconstruction To Demolition:

(The Legitimate Basis Of Demolitionism)

If anarchism and post-modernism are synonymous, then, the primary reason the post-modern age has not fully come to pass as of yet is because post-modernism has been divorced from its motor force, anarchism. Therefore, post-modernism has been sabotaged; it has been detached from its locomotive centrifuge, deep within its theoretical apparatus and critical techniques, namely, anarchism. Consequently, post-modernism has remained bourgeois, i.e., mildly critical of the meta-narrative of bourgeois-capitalism, while, simultaneously championing maximum plurality, equality and heterogeneity, via its practices. Post-modernism has fallen under the mystifying spell of bourgeois-capitalism. As a result, it has not pushed-on. Post-modernism no longer pushes forward its inherent programme for the total deconstruction of all meta-narratives, including the meta-narrative of bourgeois-capitalism. Today, post-modernism lies in maudlin stagnation, due to the fact, it is inescapably bourgeois. Having jettisoned its engine, i.e., anarchism, post-modernism has fallen into ineffective reformism. And, reformism is the system. Therefore, if post-modernism seeks to re-animate its radical critique and its revolutionary programme, and raise itself out of the sloppy stagnation it has fallen into, then, post-modernism needs to get re-acquainted with its core centrifuge, anarchism.

In effect, post-modernism has remained bourgeois by remaining trapped in the bourgeois-philosophy of mild deconstruction, that is, bourgeois-deconstruction, bourgeois-deconstruction being the careful and gradual dismantling of an apparatus or building, while, deliberately preserving certain valuable element for reuse and refurbishing. To quote, Jacques Derrida, deconstruction means "1. To disassemble the parts of a whole. To deconstruct a machine to transport elsewhere."[1] Subsequently, bourgeois-deconstruction is a gradual meticulous process, which softly and mildly, dismantles segments of a text or apparatus, while, ultimately, keeping the overall structure of a text, or structural-apparatus, intact. Derridean deconstruction dismantles a text or apparatus, but, dismantles them only to reconstruct a text or apparatus, allover again, ultimately, leaving the text or apparatus unscathed and the same as before.

Bourgeois-deconstruction makes textual structures, both conceptual and material, wobble without them falling-over or crumbling. However, according to the architect of deconstruction, Jacques Derrida, deconstruction "is neither an analysis nor a critique.[Moreover, it] is not a method and cannot be transformed into one. Deconstruction is not even an act or an operation etc."[2], it is an empty nullity. In brief, this is a retreat on Derrida's part. It is a rejection by Derrida of the revolutionary potential of deconstruction. Nevertheless, despite this retreat, by Derrida, deconstruction is most certainly all of those empowering things, i.e., it is a method, an analysis, a critique and a decisive act. Even, if Derrida plays coy and states otherwise, deconstruction embodies a certain set of rules, capable of application in a more radical manner.

First and foremost, Derrida says "deconstruction is a word"[3], and words have definitions and practical implications. Words are useful. As Ludwig Wittgenstein states, words are like "tools in a tool-box...the functions of words...serve to modify something"[4]. They have uses and this is exactly what deconstruction does, it modifies a text or structure through an analytical deconstruction process. Secondly, according to Derrida, deconstruction embodies specific instructions, instructions that stipulate that all "structures [are] to be undone, decomposed, de-sedimented... (all types of structures, linguistic, logo-centric etc.)"[5]. Consequently, despite Derrida's objections that "deconstruction [does not] correspond to some clear and univocal signification"[6], deconstruction does, nonetheless, function and operate as a philosophy and a method of analysis. It may be, as Derrida states, "an anti-structuralist gesture"[7] at its basic datum, but, deconstruction is a philosophy and a method, nonetheless, even if this philosophy is a radical form of anti-philosophy and a sort of anti-method, method.

Understanding the radical implications of deconstruction, Derrida distances himself from the concept. For instance, when asked "what is deconstruction? [Derrida responds] Nothing of course!"[8]. And, by distancing himself from the revolutionary implications of deconstruction, Derrida abandons the post-modern project of a world without grand narratives and/or large-scale oppressive discourses. By denying the revolutionary force that is deconstruction, and divorcing himself from the engine of post-modernism, anarchism, Derrida inadvertently sabotages the post-modern project and the full maturation of post-modernism. That is, Derrida sabotages the post-modern programme which demands the levelling-down of all meta-narratives in the name of maximum plurality, equality and heterogeneity, i.e., the end of large-scale oppression.

In effect, Derrida turns deconstruction into a bourgeois past-time. He de-fangs the revolutionary force inherent in deconstruction, anarchism, and domesticates deconstruction, making it tame and palpable for moderate bourgeois liberals. He turns deconstruction into a lame form of bourgeois-deconstruction. Indeed, under Derrida, deconstruction becomes a means to integrate marginal narratives and marginalized people into the meta-narrative of bourgeois-capitalism. Bourgeois-deconstruction becomes a manner by which to turn everything and everyone into bourgeois acolytes, susceptible to capitalist exploitation and capitalist domination. In short, Derrida reduces deconstruction to a form of mild, apologetic post-modernism, easily absorbed into the profit-making mechanisms of bourgeois-capitalism. Under Derrida, the concept of deconstruction becomes the concept of bourgeois-deconstruction, mild criticism and an apology for the capitalist-system.

In actuality, despite profiting from the core principles of post-modernism and anarchism, namely, radical plurality, radical equality and a radical antipathy towards all meta-narratives, Derrida sabotages these core, anarchist, post-modernist principles, by denying their factual presence within deconstruction. Derrida reduces the revolutionary implications inherent in post-modernism, anarchism and deconstruction into a mild shaking or wobbling of the dominant linguistic structures, while, in the end, always keeping them the same and intact. For example, as Derrida states, within *Grammatology*,

> The movements of deconstruction do not destroy structures. [They inhabit]....them in a certain way...operating necessarily from the inside, borrowing all the strategic and economic resources of subversion from the old structure, borrowing them structurally, [and making them wobble a little.]...[This] is...the enterprise of deconstruction.[9]

In this regard, Derrida's mild form of deconstruction reasserts, in opposition to post-modernism and anarchism, the meta-narrative of bourgeois-capitalism, by facilitating the integration of marginal groups and marginal narratives into the Enlightenment meta-narrative of bourgeois-capitalism.

The point of post-modernism and it motor force, anarchism, if one wishes to stay true to their core principles, is nothing less than the complete overthrow of all meta-narratives, especially, the meta-narrative of bourgeois-capitalism. Therefore, Derridean deconstruction is nothing more than liberal bourgeois reform. It is bourgeois in the sense that, ultimately, bourgeois-deconstruction is a mild form of domesticated deconstruction in service of the meta-narrative of bourgeois-capitalism. The result is that Derridean deconstruction fails to uphold the core tenets of post-modernism and anarchism, including deconstruction, itself. Derrida fails to follow the full-implications inherent in deconstruction to its logical conclusion, i.e., the complete overthrow of all meta-narratives.

Indeed, describing the anti-method of deconstruction at work, Gayatri Spivak, in her introduction to *Grammatology*, outlines the methodology of bourgeois deconstruction as locating

> the promising marginal text [inside the dominant text], [finding] the undecidable moment, [so as] to pry it loose ...[and] reverse the resident hierarchy, only to displace it; to dismantle [it] in order to reconstitute [it]...[Taking] away the assurance of the text's authority...by inaugurating the open-ended indefiniteness of textuality. [10]

Meaning, the point of bourgeois-deconstruction is not the demolition of meta-narratives and oppressive structures, the point is to make these meta-narratives and oppressive structures wobble, while, ultimately keeping them intact in hopes that these oppressive structures and meta-narratives will open-up themselves to a broader inclusion of marginal groups and narratives.

In the final analysis, the point of Derridean bourgeois-deconstruction is merely to cast doubt on a text or apparatus, whether, this text or apparatus is conceptual or material. The hope is to cast doubt on these ruling conceptual and material structures in order to permit the integration of marginal groups and perspectives into the meta-narrative of bourgeois-capitalism. Consequently, Derridean deconstruction is a form of reformism, already a mechanism of the bourgeois system, designed to defuse any revolutionary fervor against the bourgeois system through integration.

In fact, Derrida never mentions the revolutionary implications of deconstruction, specifically, the implication that if there is a complete lack of foundation, or solid ground, underlying any meta-authority, since, "there is [no] pure signified"[11], then, there is no such thing as ultimate truth, or being. There is in essence no timeless meta-authority by which to judge, equitably and impartially any text or apparatus. Meaning, there is no legitimate or justifiable ground for the governing power of any meta-authority, whatsoever. This is the unstated radical implications of deconstruction.

Moreover, following the logic of deconstruction to its logical conclusion, this means there is legitimate reason or justifiable evidence to eliminate all meta-authorities from the face of the earth, on grounds that they are unjustifiable, unfounded, arbitrary authority figures. Following the logic of deconstruction to its logical conclusion, the only justifiable and legitimate authority possible, which can reflect a certain level of legitimacy is a decentralized patchwork of micro-narratives and individuals, namely, a plurality of micro-narratives and individuals sharing decision-making-authority, equally, between themselves, unopposed, by any overarching, authoritarian meta-narrative. The revolutionary implications of deconstruction is that the only possible socio-economic formation capable of real legitimacy is some form of socio-economic heterogeneity and radical equality for all.

Therefore, Derridean deconstruction is inescapably bourgeois, because, it is buttresses the meta-narrative of bourgeois-capitalism, it does not deconstruct any meta-authority beyond the point of no return, hence, the reason it is bourgeois. Derridean bourgeois-deconstruction is still around because it is useful to bourgeois-capitalism in that it expands its dominion and its control over the micro-recesses of everyday life and the general-population, by encouraging the integration of marginalized narratives, moments of everyday life, and segments of the general-population within the bourgeois totalitarian framework.

The only solution to Derrida's mild form of docile, obedient deconstruction is that it must be completely abandoned. The revolutionary implications of deconstruction must be extracted, radicalized and turned into a form of conceptual and material demolitionism, while, the Derridean practice of mild deconstruction must be jettisoned to the dust-bin of history and replaced by demolitionism. Demolitionism is the logic of deconstruction pushed to its ultimate conclusion, demolition. Demolitionism is a radical form of deconstruction bent on the total demolition of all meta-narratives, especially, the meta-narrative of bourgeois-capitalism.

So, demolitionism is both a radical critique of Derridean bourgeois-deconstruction and a radical outgrowth of Derridean deconstruction. It is a pragmatic methodology and praxis, both conceptual and material, which fully embodies the core principles of post-modernism and anarchism. Demolitionism uncompromisingly demands the complete tear-down or demolition of all meta-narratives, including the meta-narrative of bourgeois-capitalism, in all shapes and forms. Demolitionism does not stop at the mild shaking or questioning of the dominant conceptual and material structures of bourgeois-capitalism, as Derrida does, instead, demolitionism is a process and radical critique, designed for the total demolition of the dominant conceptual and material structures of bourgeois-capitalism in service of radical post-modernism and radical anarchism. It is demolition in the name of equality, diversity and heterogeneity.

In league with Bakunin, demolitionism "requires an extensive and widespread destruction, a fecund and renovating destruction, since in this way and only this way are new worlds born"[12]. Demolitionism is the "elemental force [of anarchist post-modernism designed to] sweep... away all [despotic] obstacles"[13]. Demolitionism is, in essence, a pragmatic radical form of deconstruction, both material and conceptual, programmed to detonate all meta-narratives sky-high. The objective is to clear the way for radical plurality, radical equality, and multi-varied anarchist post-modernity, wherefore, decision-making-authority is shared between all micro-narratives, in relative equal measure. The objective of demolitionism is to establish a clearing for the full-development of post-modernism, that is, for the full-development of post-modern anarchism.

In sum, demolitionism is the anti-method of radical plurality, radical equality, namely, the radical tear-down of all meta-narratives. The point of demolitionism is to permit a plethora of micro-narratives to flourish and thrive in the bosom of a fully-developed post-modern age. That is, a post-modern anarchist society, without the presence of any ruling meta-authority determining relations and narrative organizations. As a result, at its core, demolitionism is "the vengeance of the oppressed"[14]; it is an instrument of radical equality, affirming, on legitimate grounds,"by all means, let us destroy! [And,] let us demolish!"[15].

Endnotes:

[1] Jacques Derrida, *"Letter to a Japanese Friend", A Derrida Reader (Between The Blinds)*, ed. Peggy Kamuf, (New York: Columbia University Press, 1991) p. 271.
[2] Ibid, p. 273.
[3] Ibid, p. 275.
[4] Ludwig Wittgenstein, *Philosophical Investigations*, Trans. G.E.M. Anscombe, (New Jersey: Prentice Hall, 1958) pp. 6-7.
[5] Jacques Derrida, *"Letter to a Japanese Friend", A Derrida Reader (Between The Blinds)*, ed. Peggy Kamuf, (New York: Columbia University Press, 1991) p. 272.
[6] Ibid, p. 270.
[7] Ibid, p. 272.
[8] Ibid, p. 275.
[9] Jacques Derrida, *Of Grammatology*, Trans. Gayatri Spivak (Baltimore: Johns Hopkins University Press, 2016) p. 25.
[10] Ibid, pp. c-ci.
[11] Ibid, p. 174.
[12] Mikhail Bakunin, *Bakunin On Anarchy*, ed. Sam Dolgoff, (New York: Vintage Books, 1972) p. 334.
[13] Ibid, p. 325.
[14] Errico Malatesta, *Errico Malatesta: His Life and Ideas*, ed. Vernon Richards, (London: Freedom Press, 1984) p. 477.
[15] Ibid, p. 475.

Ch.3:

Post-Modernism Has Not Yet Smashed To Pieces The Meta-Narrative Of Bourgeois-Capitalism:

(Why post-modernism has not fully bloomed & Why bourgeois-capitalism rules over plurality)

Western, high-tech. civilization can never fully enter the post-modern era, without eradicating civilization of bourgeois-state-capitalism, namely, the meta-narrative of bourgeois-capitalism. That is, that encrusted jewel, dead-center, within the crown of the Enlightenment, which continues to infect and poison high-tech. society with a most horrible sickness, insatiable avarice, an avarice for unlimited power, profit and money. The post-modern era cannot achieve full-maturity under, current, bourgeois-capitalism conditions as the grand-narrative of bourgeois-capitalism continually impedes the overwhelming diversity, equality, and plurality, post-modernity and anarchism champion and inherently demand. In effect, post-modernism has not yet smashed to pieces all the grand-narratives of the Enlightenment, specifically, bourgeois-capitalism, which continues to stalk the bright and the dark corners of western civilization, weaving and grafting in-commensurable global and local narratives into a massive totalitarian meta-narrative, called, the logic of bourgeois-capitalism.

Contrary to Jean-Francois Lyotard, "the principle of a plurality of [linguistic] systems"[1], existing side by side, in in-commensurable independence, without any overarching meta-narrative terrorizing over the others, in service of heterogeneity and equality, is false and nonsense. It is false and nonsense because bourgeois-capitalism encroaches upon every aspect of everyday life, stitching any sort of in-commensurable narrative into a functionalist-capitalist dominion. That is, a dominion, whose fundamental imperative is the profit-imperative, i.e., the logic of capitalism, which commands, "the maximization of profit, by any means necessary, at the lowest financial cost, as soon as possible"[2], regardless of the type of narrative, big or small. Specifically, the post-modern age has not come to pass as of yet as the Enlightenment meta-narrative of bourgeois-capitalism persists relatively unopposed.

For Lyotard, the primary characteristic of the post-modern age, i.e., the post-modern condition, is that "grand narrative[s] [have] lost…credibility" [3] and that "the decline of [meta-narratives] can be seen as an effect of the development of techniques and technologies, since the Second World War" [4], which, according to Lyotard, have vanquished the Enlightenment and its meta-narratives to the social periphery and reduced society to a matter of money, profit and "the logic of maximum performance"[5]. That is, the maximum performance in achieving maximum power and maximum capitalist profitability in and across everyday life and socio-economic existence, wherein, a select few, exemplify the logic of capitalism in all its opulent splendor, reaping all its rewards. This lucky select few, in effect, congeal into a state-finance-corporate-aristocracy.

According to Jean Francois Lyotard, the dissolution and de-legitimization of grand-narratives, due to technological progress, which is constantly moving in "the direction [of]…the computerization of society" [6], has meant "a loss of meaning"[7] across high-tech. western civilization. In effect, the ever-increasing accumulation of techno-scientific knowledge and autonomous technologies has increasingly undermined age old certainties, wherefore, according to Marx, "all fast-frozen relations…are swept away [and] all that is solid melts into air…[whereupon] man is at last compelled to face with sober senses, his real conditions of life"[8], bourgeois-money and bourgeois-power-relations.

This capitalist techno-scientific process is a process of creative-destruction. According to Joseph Schumpeter, this is "the essential fact about capitalism"[9]. Through the techno-scientific process of creative-destruction a sense of demoralization and skepticism has set-in across high-tech. Civilization. The result is that all great social and communal aims pertaining to the Enlightenment myths have fallen into disrepute, as everything, as everyone, and as every technological process, increasingly boils down to "optimizing the [capitalist] system's performance"[10]. The fact is that the optimization of capitalist performance, invariably, always revolves around maximizing capitalist profit and capitalist power, at the expense of other possible performance objectives, which are, in effect, cast aside. As a result, for Schumpeter, bourgeois-capitalism incessantly produces an "atmosphere of almost universal hostility to its own social order"[11]. In essence, bourgeois-capitalism, through its constant mechanism of creative-destruction, manufactures "an atmosphere of hostility [that] decomposes the… forces of capitalism from within"[12], undermining the very mode of production that capitalism relies upon, namely, the capitalist mode of production. Specifically, the capitalist mode of production can be described as a specific social-relation fused with certain forces of production. It is the capital/labor relation, where, capital dominates labor in a certain format laid-out around certain forces of production. The point is to produce profit and capital for a select few, who enjoy the bulk of benefits derived from this relation of domination between capital and labor.

Notwithstanding, like Schumpeter, for Lyotard, "capitalism…cannot exist without a [constant] shattering of belief and [a]…the lack of [firm] reality" [13], due to the fact that bourgeois-capitalism requires a certain amount of vacuity, both mental and physical, in order to establish its own capitalist categories and economic realities. These capitalist categories and realities are artificially constructed in order to maximize capitalist profits, capitalist power, and establish capitalism as best and most legitimate socio-economic system in the eyes of the general-population. Even if this is, in reality, false and/or false-consciousness. The point, for bourgeois-capitalism, is to encourage nihilism in and across everyday life, that is, "the conviction of the [unattainability] of… [universal] values [which in turn seed] …the idea of valueless-ness [and] meaninglessness…[across] existence" [14]. The point of manufacturing nihilism is to open opportunities in and across everyday life for capitalist commodities to fill the void manifested by this man-made nihilism.

However, this manufactured nihilism, according to Schumpeter, simultaneously manifests a universal hostility towards capitalism in the sense that "after having destroyed the moral authority of so many other [non-capitalist] institutions, [capitalism] … turns against its own [institutions]"[15], and corrodes its own structures and relations. In effect, the mechanisms of bourgeois-capitalism, designed to maintain and perpetuate the Enlightenment meta-narrative of bourgeois-capitalism, ad infinitum, also corrode the very faith in the supremacy of bourgeois-state-capitalism in the name of capitalist profit. Nihilism is the result. And, the remedy bourgeois-capitalism offers to fill the void of rampant nihilism is commodities, endless capitalist commodities.

Consequently, according to Lyotard, capitalist-techno-science reduces, and continuously reduces, human existence to a series of power "moves" founded on the accumulation of wealth, influence, and increased performativity, all of which, demolish grand-narratives and produce nihilism as an after-effect. In fact, for Lyotard, nihilism results from

> this breaking up of the grand narratives [which leads to] the dissolution of the social bond and the disintegration of social aggregates into a mass of individual atoms thrown into [constant]...motion. [Whereupon], each [individualist atom now] exists in a fabric of relations that is now more complex and mobile than ever before. [In fact,] young or old, man or woman, rich or poor, ...is [now] always located at [various] nodal points of specific communication circuits, however tiny these may be. [However, the point of this is]...to improve...[systemic, capitalist] performance. [16]

With every technological intrusion and amelioration, in and across everyday life, the sum of socio-economic existence is atomized to its smallest unit possible. Wherefore, belief in anything transcendent is shattered and "the goal is no longer truth, but performativity"[17], namely, the maximization of profit and power in the hands of a select few, which compose the upper-echelons of the capitalist-system.

And, the only life-line offered, by bourgeois-capitalism, after the dissolution of meta-narratives, according to Lyotard, is the empty-transcendence offered through the consumption of capitalist commodities, which, in the end, exacerbate the prevalent feeling of emptiness, pervading the stratums of everyday life. As a result of this emptying-out process, "the only credible goal [becomes] power"[18] within the parameters of bourgeois-state-capitalism.

Technology reduces socio-economic existence and everyday life to means/ends rationality, i.e., the functional imperative, which focuses on the maximization of power and capital, where "the question… now asked by…the State, [people,] or institutions…is no longer is it true, but, what use is it?...[and] is it saleable?...[that is] is it efficient?" [19]. This reductive process, brought about via technological progress under bourgeois-capitalism, means that "we no longer have recourse to grand-narratives. We can resort neither to the dialectic of spirit nor even to the emancipation of humanity as [our] validation [for anything]"[20]. Faith and belief crumble into disillusionment, alienation and, finally, the dead-end of universal nihilism.

Everything, every process, becomes a matter of maximizing power and profit, "the social system [is] conceived as a totality in quest of its most performative unity possible"[21]. And, like cogs in a machine, humans are utilized to ameliorate the system's performativity and augment capitalist profit. As Lyotard states, "the [capitalist] system seems to be a vanguard machine dragging humanity after it, dehumanizing it in order to re-humanize it at a different level of [socio-economic] capacity, [via managing] technocrats"[22]. That is, technocrats which administrate "individuals [to] want what the [capitalist] system needs in order to perform well"[23].

However, for Lyotard, post-modernism is "un fait accompli", it is already here in full bloom, but clearly, Lyotard, cunningly smuggles into his description of the post-modern condition, the meta-narrative of bourgeois-capitalism, in the sense that every process, every plurality, everything in his description of the post-modern condition revolves around the maximization of capitalist performance and the accumulation of capitalist profits. Consequently, Lyotard, when describing the post-modern condition is constantly caught in the tension of the meta-narrative of bourgeois-capitalism and the advent of post-modernism. That is, of having to describe totalitarian bourgeois-capitalism, simultaneously, as he champions the dissolution of meta-narratives and the rise of radical plurality and equality.

Granted, the Enlightenment grand-narratives of social emancipation and spirit, i.e., the quest for absolute knowledge and freedom, have faded and lost credibility, as Lyotard argues, but, nonetheless, the Enlightenment grand-narrative of bourgeois-capitalism persists and, in fact, has filled the void, left behind, by these other Enlightenment grand-narratives. According to Lyotard, the "post-modern [is]...the condition [where there is]...no regulating [universal] ideal"[24], yet, this is not the case in the sense that the Enlightenment meta-narrative of bourgeois-capitalism has become the new universal ideal, determining the direction of high-tech. western civilization and its ruling narratives.

Indeed, the meta-narrative of bourgeois-capitalism enables the domination of certain capitalist judgments and capitalist criterions, which continue to establish bourgeois social norms and capitalist existential standards, in and across the stratums of everyday life on behalf of the old grand-narratives of the Enlightenment. As Lyotard states, with sleight of hand, "capitalism...disguises its 'realism' under the idea of an emancipation from poverty"[25], wherefore, once again, the Enlightenment meta-narrative of human emancipation is covertly reintroduced under the new disguise of bourgeois-capitalism, which establishes "the [Enlightenment] economic genre...[as the] universal criterion" [26]. The result is that the universal "tribunal of capitalism's...verdict [is] always pronounced in favor of [profit and power]" [27], namely, bourgeois-money, bourgeois-property and bourgeois-power.

Moreover, the sensus communis, i.e., the sense of community, which Lyotard states has disappeared across high-tech. western civilization, due to the dissolution of the grand-narratives of emancipation and absolute

Spirit/knowledge, is reintroduced via the meta-narrative of bourgeois-capitalism, which imposes a new social bond on social relations, founded on systemic performativity, bourgeois-money, bourgeois-property and bourgeois-power. This forceful intrusion of bourgeois-capitalism, on behalf of the Enlightenment, annuls Lyotard's post-modern notion of any federation of infinite, in-commensurable micro-narratives, interacting with each other, devoid of an overarching or dominant meta-logic. Indeed, undermining his own argument, Lyotard readily states,

> the economic genre [of bourgeois-capitalism has] hegemony over the others, [it] can...put on the garb of an emancipatory philosophy of history, [imposing the idea of] more wealth. The economic genre of capital in no way requires... [to] admit...heterogeneity. To the contrary, it requires the suppression of that heterogeneity.[28]

Lyotard seems to be perpetrating a ruse in the sense that he is arguing for two simultaneous contradictory positions, which are, in fact, diametrically opposed positions, namely, polar oppositions. That is, Lyotard is simultaneously arguing 1. that the heterogeneity of micro-narratives, devoid of any unifying principles and/or meta-narratives is the new condition of socio-economic existence found in and across western high-tech. civilization, namely, post-modernity, while, simultaneously, arguing 2. that bourgeois-capitalism holds hegemony over all these in-commensurable micro-narratives, in and across western high-tech. civilization.

In fact, Lyotard readily states in the quotation above that the meta-narrative of bourgeois-capitalism suppresses the sum of heterogeneous micro-narratives, phrases and/or language-games, in favor of maximum performance, maximum power, and maximum capital, which directly contradicts his idea of the prevalence of heterogeneous, post-modernity. The fact that there are no longer any universal criterias to base judgments upon, but instead, a vast plethora of pluralities. Post-modern heterogeneity is seriously curtailed and limited by the hegemony and homogeneity of bourgeois-capitalism, which is imposed its ruling world view and capitalist hierarchies upon the plurality of micro-narratives, including the egalitarianism of post-modernism.

Although, Lyotard states, we need not concern ourselves too much about the encroachment of the meta-narrative of bourgeois-capitalism, since, bourgeois-capitalist "bureaucratization is [merely an] outer limit"[29], nevertheless, there is still an application of force being applied to corral in-commensurable micro-narratives into a unity. As he states, despite the fact that "today…the limits [that any bourgeois-capitalist] institution imposes on… language [and language] 'moves', [these] are never established once and for all"[30]. For Lyotard, micro-narratives are free despite continually being subjugated by the Enlightenment meta-narrative of bourgeois-capitalism. Basically, Lyotard, brushes aside, with a gentle sleight of hand, the fact that there is still an Enlightenment meta-narrative at work, controlling "the flexible networks of language games"[31].

This is a disingenuous contradiction by Lyotard. He argues that, despite the dominance of the meta-narrative of bourgeois-capitalism, its control is soft, pliable, and never truly finalized in the sense that the limits which bourgeois-capitalism places onto the strands of micro-narratives are always subject to change. They are merely stakes in all narrative confrontations. Nevertheless, by Lyotard's own admission, the Enlightenment's meta-narratives continue to influence, control, and impose, limits on plurality, diversity, and egalitarianism. In the end, the radical equality of post-modernism, Lyotard describes, is abolished by the despotism of bourgeois-capitalism which imposes upon the plurality and equality of micro-narratives, totalitarian unity. As a result, post-modernism is incomplete, it is suppressed. It is suppressed because it is divorced from its motor force, anarchism. The meta-narrative of bourgeois-capitalism has divorced post-modernism from its engine, anarchism. Hence, the reason why post-modernism is incomplete, truncated and unfinished.

For Lyotard, the post-modern condition is more or less a condition, exclusively, consigned to the upper-echelons of bourgeois-capitalism, i.e., capitalist technocrats and capitalist decision-makers, who comprise the most indoctrinated and profit-driven social groupings in and across the system of bourgeois-capitalism. As he states,

> What is a good…utterance, a 'good' performance in…technical matters? They are all judged to be 'good' because they conform to the relevant [bourgeois-capitalist] criteria (of justice, beauty, truth, and efficiency respectively) accepted in the social circles of [anointed capitalist] knowers.[32]

These anointed capitalist knowers are chosen by the best proponents of the Enlightenment meta-narrative of bourgeois-capitalism. These anointed capitalist knowers are the embodiment of the meta-narrative of bourgeois-capitalism, meant to spread the gospel of bourgeois-capitalism and befuddle any opposing criterions of judgment, which may run contrary to the meta-narrative of bourgeois-capitalism.

For Lyotard, the play, the flexibility, and the diversity, expressed in the plurality of micro-narratives, devoid of meta-narratives, are exclusively consigned to, and safeguarded for, the upper-echelons of bourgeois-state-capitalism. That is, where the capitalist system's imperative for maximum systemic performance and profit, does not apply. In a similar fashion, Marx always argued that the best exemplars of bourgeois-capitalism never apply the same criteria to themselves which they apply to the workforce/population, in general. As Marx states, "the non-worker does everything against the worker which the worker does against him/herself, but he [or she] does not do against him/herself what he [or she] does against the worker" [33]. Meaning, that the best exemplars of the meta-narrative of bourgeois-capitalism hold themselves to a different standard and criteria than they hold and apply against the workforce/population. They solely apply the rigors of the logic of capitalism and the logic of optimum performance to the workforce/population, while, excusing themselves from such a criterion and imperatives.

Consequently, the bourgeois imperative of optimum capitalist performance and profit is an imperative imposed upon the lower stratums of the capitalist-system, both forcefully and softly, whereupon, the general-population continually has to perform and conform to what "the principle of optimal [capitalist] performance [and profit]"[34] demand and/or command. There are no exceptions. The upper-echelons of bourgeois-capitalism are absolved of these imperatives, their task is to manage western high-tech. civilization, unencumbered, along the lines of the logic of capitalism, i.e., the capitalist performance criterions. Specifically, by being exempt from the rigors of this maximum performance imperative, there lot is merely to enjoy the fruits and the luxuries that this capitalist performance criterion, i.e., profit-imperative, provides them, while, crushing the emancipation of any micro-narratives, which might be antithetic to bourgeois-capitalism.

In this regard, the Enlightenment endures through the empty Utopian promises of universal bourgeois-capitalism, which as Lyotard states, celebrate a form of post-modern eclecticism, with a certain sense of liberty and infinite choice, when this, in fact, is not truly the case. It is not the case in the sense that this so-called post-modern eclecticism, celebrating liberty and choice, is without real socio-economic diversity, equality, and linguistic heterogeneity. It is an eclecticism based upon monetary power, namely, purchasing power.

As always, money talks and money is all that matters, such is the essential imperative lodged inside the grand-narrative of bourgeois-capitalism. In actuality, bourgeois post-modernity is a superficial diversity, equality, and heterogeneity, localized primarily in capitalist commodities, which demand that for anyone to participate in this eclectic bourgeois façade and capitalist pageantry, they must possess a certain level of monetary-power. Indeed, Lyotard is correct, when he states,

> postmodern…eclecticism is the degree zero of contemporary general culture: [where] one listens to reggae, watches a western, eats McDonald's food for lunch and local cuisine for dinner, wears Paris perfume in Tokyo and "retro" clothes in Hong Kong…[and] "anything goes". The epoch is one of slackening…but this realism of "anything goes" is in fact that of money [where the] criteria…to assess…value [is based on] profits and…purchasing power. [35]

Insofar, as the meta-narrative of bourgeois-capitalism promises to satisfy all human needs via an incessant celebratory monologue that champions the capitalist marketplace, the catch, or ruse, is the fact that these human needs must first have a certain level of power and money in order to be acknowledged as valid needs, pertaining to the governing meta-narrative of bourgeois-capitalism.

Consequently, the post-modern epoch maybe defined as an infinite series of in-commensurable language-games and discourses etc., by Lyotard, however, these in-commensurable language-games and discourses are, nonetheless, continuously unified and tied together via the meta-narrative of bourgeois-capitalism, which through "the exercise of terror…says 'adapt your aspiration to our [capitalist] ends –or else" [36]. The exercise of terror, by the Enlightenment meta-narrative of bourgeois-capitalism, imposes a unifying principle, or profit-imperative, upon the plurality of language-games, discourses, and narratives, ultimately, impeding the development, the maturation, and the full-realization of post-modernism, through the exercise of a certain form of bourgeois-capitalist terrorism. That is, a very real fear, threatening the multiplicity of language-games, narratives, and discourses, with imprisonment, unemployment, repression, hunger or worst etc., if there is too much deviation between them, or between them and the meta-narrative of bourgeois-capitalism.

In consequence, the despotism imposed by the meta-narrative of bourgeois-capitalism "does not respect the plurality of language-games"[37], but instead, imposes a totalitarian regime upon post-modernism, which distorts, falsifies, and misrepresents, its fundamental goal and imperative: egalitarianism and anarchism. That is, egalitarianism and anarchism, in all shapes and forms, which demand plurality, diversity, and socio-economic equality, in relative equal measure, for all micro-narratives in and across all stratums of everyday life, regardless of race, gender, class, age or background etc.

As a result, the actualization of post-modernity is stifled by the meta-narrative of bourgeois-capitalism. It is cut short. It is divorced from its motor force, anarchism. It is asphyxiated in the name of bourgeois-power, bourgeois-profits and bourgeois-money, namely, the last standing grand-narrative of the Enlightenment, bourgeois-state-capitalism, which favors only those who best embody, represent, and exemplify, the meta-narrative of bourgeois-capitalism, i.e., bourgeois-capitalist money, bourgeois-capitalist power and bourgeois-capitalist property.

In fact, Lyotard readily admits in his limited version of post-modernity, outlined in *The Post-modern Condition*, that the bourgeois-capitalist "ruling class is and will continue to be the class of decision makers. [Namely] …[that the] composite layer of corporate leaders, high-level administrators and the heads of the major professional, labor, political and religious organizations"[38], will continue to enact their judgments and their influence in service of the Enlightenment meta-narrative of bourgeois-capitalism. In this regard, Lyotard puts forward a false-view of post-modernism, that is, a view of post-modernism, which champions plurality, equality, and egalitarianism, while, simultaneously, still being ruled by a cadre of bourgeois-capitalist aristocrats and technocrats, i.e., a state-finance-corporate-aristocracy. As a result, there can be no genuine plurality of micro-narratives, when, the unitary meta-narrative of bourgeois-capitalism suppresses this plurality in the name of unity and homogenization.

Ultimately, what Lyotard fails to mention is that post-modernity has not fully bloomed, i.e., that it has not gone far enough; insofar as it has yet to realize its raison d'être, total egalitarianism, in its utmost capacity. Post-modernism has not gone far enough, due to the fact that the seeming plurality of language-games, discourses, phrases, and micro-narratives, pervading everyday life, continues to be suppressed under the ever-lingering, Enlightenment meta-narrative of bourgeois-capitalism.

Post-modernism has not fully realized as of yet that it is anarchism in theoretical form, while, anarchism has not fully realized as of yet that it is post-modernism in pragmatic, practical form. So, as Lyotard states, "the price to pay for such…illusions is terror" [39]. Namely, the forceful application of a set of bourgeois-capitalist criterias, by the meta-narrative of bourgeois-capitalism, onto all micro-narratives so as to impede the full-realization of the post-modern anarchist principles of radical plurality, radical equality, and radical demolitionism, which are shared by both post-modernism and anarchism.

In sum, the meta-narrative of bourgeois-capitalism has filled the void left-over by those other obsolete, Enlightenment meta-narratives, described by Lyotard, the grand-narrative of absolute knowledge and the grand-narrative of human emancipation etc., however, like them, the meta-narrative of bourgeois-capitalism perpetuates covertly the universal ideals of the Enlightenment. As a result, despite the "nation-states, parties, professions, institutions, and historical traditions…losing their attraction"[40], like a zombie, the Enlightenment meta-narrative of bourgeois-capitalism lingers-on and persists in imposing its despotism over all micro-narratives. That is, the Enlightenment persists in fashioning "society [into] a unified totality,…[a] perfectly sealed circle of facts…[that is, a] social whole [programmed] for the optimization of… [capitalist] performance"[41]. Consequently, if post-modernism is to achieve full maturity, it is imperative that all small micro-narratives, in anarchist fashion, "wage war on totality [and seek to] activate [and multiply] differences"[42], in every shape and form. The meta-narrative of bourgeois-capitalism can only be nullified and smashed into a million pieces through the conceptual and material fusion of anarchism and post-modernism, in unison, exercising systematic demolitionism.

Endnotes:

[1] Jean-Francois Lyotard, *The Post-Modern Condition*, Trans. Geoff Bennington and Brian Massimo (Minneapolis: University of Minnesota Press, 1984) p. 43.

[2] Michel Luc Bellemare, *The Structural-Anarchism Manifesto*: *(The Logic of Structural-Anarchism Versus The Logic of Capitalism)*, (Montréal: Blacksatin Publications Inc., 2016) p. 6.b.

[3] Jean-Francois Lyotard, *The Post-Modern Condition*, Trans. Geoff Bennington and Brian Massimo (Minneapolis: University of Minnesota Press, 1984) p. 37.

[4] Ibid, p. 37.

[5] Ibid, p. xxxiv.

[6] Ibid, p. 7.

[7] Ibid, p. 26.

[8] Karl Marx, *"Manifesto of the Communist Party", The Marx-Engels Reader*, Ed. Robert C. Tucker (New York, New York: W.W. Norton & Company Inc., 1978) p. 476.

[9] Joseph A. Schumpeter, *Can Capitalism Survive? (Creative Destruction and The Future of The Global Economy)*, (New York, New York: Harper & Row, 1950) p. 43.

[10] Jean-Francois Lyotard, *The Post-Modern Condition*, Trans.Geoff Bennington and Brian Massimo (Minneapolis: University of Minnesota Press, 1984) p. xxiv.

[11] Joseph A. Schumpeter, *Can Capitalism Survive? (Creative Destruction and The Future of The Global Economy)*, (New York, New York: Harper & Row, 1950) p. 155.

[12] Ibid, p. 191.

[13] Jean-Francois Lyotard, *The Post-Modern Condition*, Trans. Geoff Bennington and Brian Massimo (Minneapolis: University of Minnesota Press, 1984) p. 77.
[14] Friedrich Nietzsche, *The Will To Power*, Ed. Walter Kaufmann (New York, New York: Vintage Books, 1967) pp. 9-11.
[15] Joseph A. Schumpeter, *Can Capitalism Survive? (Creative Destruction and The Future of The Global Economy)*, (New York, New York: Harper & Row, 1950) pp. 155-156.
[16] Jean-Francois Lyotard, *The Post-Modern Condition*, Trans. Geoff Bennington and Brian Massimo (Minneapolis: University of Minnesota Press, 1984) p. 15.
[17] Ibid, p. 46.
[18] Ibid, p. 46.
[19] Ibid, p. 51.
[20] Ibid, p. 60.
[21] Ibid, p. 63.
[22] Ibid, p. 63.
[23] Ibid, p. 62.
[24] Jean-Francois Lyotard and Jean-Loup Thebaud, *Just Gaming*, Trans. Wlad Godzich, (Minneapolis: University of Minnesota Press, 1985) p. 16.
[25] Jean-Francois Lyotard, *The Differend: Phrases in Dispute*, Trans. Georges Van Den Abbeele (Minneapolis: University of Minnesota Press, 1988) p. 155.
[26] Ibid, p. 177.
[27] Ibid, p. 178.
[28] Ibid, p. 178.

[29] Jean-Francois Lyotard, *The Post-Modern Condition*, Trans. Geoff Bennington and Brian Massimo (Minneapolis: University of Minnesota Press, 1984) p. 17.

[30] Ibid, p. 17.

[31] Ibid, p. 17.

[32] Ibid, p. 19.

[33] Karl Marx, *"Economic and Philosophic Manuscripts of 1844", The Marx-Engels Reader*, ed. Robert C. Tucker (New York, New York: W.W. Norton & Company Inc., 1978) p. 81.

[34] Jean-Francois Lyotard, *The Post-Modern Condition*, Trans. Geoff Bennington and Brian Massimo (Minneapolis: University of Minnesota Press, 1984) p. 44.

[35] Ibid, p. 76.

[36] Ibid, p. 64.

[37] Jean-Francois Lyotard and Jean-Loup Thebaud, *Just Gaming*, Trans. Wlad Godzich (Minneapolis: University of Minnesota Press, 1985) p. 98.

[38] Jean-Francois Lyotard, *The Post-Modern Condition*, Trans. Geoff Bennington and Brian Massimo (Minneapolis: University of Minnesota Press, 1984) p. 14.

[39] Ibid, p. 81,

[40] Ibid, p. 14.

[41] Ibid, p. 12.

[42] Ibid, p. 82.

Ch.4:

Post-Modernism Does Not Go Far Enough!

(An Argument For Pragmatic-Egalitarianism & The End of Bourgeois-Capitalism)

Post-modernism, without anarchism, does not go far enough! It has not overturned all meta-narratives and fully established its essence, that is, a multiplicity of micro-narratives, achieved through a radical "incredulity toward meta-narratives" [1]. Consequently, post-modernism has yet to realize the post-modern society, that is, a patchwork/federation of localized, decentralized, and horizontalized micro-institutions, founded on a litany of microscopic, narratives and ideational comprehensive frameworks (ideologies), where none fully dominates and terrorizes over the others. If post-modernism can be defined as a socio-economic framework where "there are no criterias"[2], where "there is no longer any…[overarching] system of rules" [3], and where "there is no [universal] sensus communis" [4], then, post-modernism has only partially succeeded. The reason being that the Enlightenment meta-narrative of bourgeois-capitalism continues to weave all the seemingly, independent micro-narratives or ideational comprehensive frameworks, together, into a cohesive whole, that is, a totalitarian bourgeois-capitalist unity.

In effect, the Enlightenment meta-narrative of bourgeois-capitalism homogenizes and unifies the diversity and the multiplicity of micro-narratives into a totality. That is, a bourgeois-capitalist totality which post-modernism seeks to abolish and/or overturn, but, cannot due to the fact that it has not materialized its critique, namely, anarchism. As a result, post-modernism has not realized its raison d'être, i.e., "a federation of municipalities, cooperatives and autonomous-collectives. That is, a plurality sharing, in egalitarian fashion, decision-making-authority, ownership, knowledge, and the sum of capital" [5], where "all… positions [or narratives] are equivalent" [6] and no-one micro-narrative "imposes itself upon the others, [and] sets itself up as dominant…[while] reducing…the multiplicity to silence" [7]. So, the reason the anarchist patchwork/federation has not come about is that post-modernism has not reached its Nth degree, wherein, it manifests its essence, i.e., anarchism, and transforms itself into anarchist post-modernism in action. Namely, it has not activated its practical methodology, anarchism. That is, total pragmatic demolition, wherein, a post-modern "imaginative activism…[is] used in various [manners for the total]…de-sedimentation"[8] of bourgeois-capitalism. The point of post-modernism is physical and mental demolitionism of all grand-institutional structures, which have grown out of, and enshrined, the Enlightenment meta-narrative of bourgeois-capitalism. Consequently, post-modernism has interpreted the world, but it has not sought to truly change it, that is, to act upon its conclusions, with a certain pluralized authority. Post-modernism has not attained its apex, i.e., pragmatic criticism, active anarchism.

Therefore, the result of the current strands of post-modernism are nothing but a re-fortification of the Enlightenment and its modern capitalist hierarchies. The result is a furthering of the convoluted minutia of arbitrary rules and regulations designed to maintain the bourgeois aristocracy and the outdated, bourgeois-capitalist status quo, which in fact, today, impedes evermore intellectual and material advancement.

In effect, these arbitrary bourgeois rules and regulations have no actual validity and are solely designed to enforce an outdated bourgeois-capitalist status quo, through, a litany of irrational divisions, which serve no other purpose other than impeding intellectual and material advancement, because these advancements embody and promote collectivism, egalitarianism, and the overthrow of the capitalist-hierarchical status quo. Today, all "grand-narratives [have] lost…credibility"[9], yet, the grand-narrative of bourgeois-state-capitalism, as socio-economic savior, continues to persist and weave the litany of independent micro-narratives into a cohesive totality, by force, by money and by political machination.

Notwithstanding, after post-modernism and its scathing critique, there is no valid, or legitimate, argument for not establishing complete financial equality, collectivism, and total social egalitarianism, due to the fact that "there is not a single---logic---that underlies all…domains"[10]. Meaning, that all micro-narratives have legitimate claim to resources, moreover, including the fact that such an egalitarian redistribution of resources would in actuality maximize opportunities for intellectual and material advancement. Bourgeois-capitalism and bourgeois-ideology impede the intellectual and material advancement of the human species because bourgeois-capitalism and bourgeois-ideology "silence people…forbidding them to speak [if they are not proponents of bourgeois-capitalism. As a result] knowledge production and knowledge distribution [are not]…free" [11]. These things are curtailed and contained within a bourgeois-capitalist framework, which excludes many participants and points of views, due to the fact they are anti-bourgeois and anti-capitalist in nature.

After post-modernism and its scathing critique, there is no such thing as the legitimate ownership of capital, money and/or private property, as in actuality, everyone has legitimate claim, in relative equal measure, upon all property, all capital, all money, and moreover, should all have access, equally to all property, all capital and all money. The reason being the fact, "knowledge is obtained by a multiplicity of views rather from the determined application of a preferred ideology"[12]. That is, because "there is no meta-language... [which can] ground political and ethical decisions"[13], then, all micro-narratives have legitimate claim, in relative equal measure, upon all socio-economic resources within society, since, there is no legitimate, rightful, universal position for any judgments. That is, "there is no stable system to guide [and legitimize] judgments"[14].

In a world where truth and judgment are relative, all positions and viewpoints are equally valid and, rightfully, entitled to an equal distribution of socio-economic resources. Therefore, the point of post-modernism, and anarchism, is to encourage, promote, and build a plurality, i.e., "a complex [of] heterogeneous historical processes [and frameworks]"[15] which can maximize intellectual and material advancement, by permitting equal access to all socio-economic resources, in relative equal measure, for all. Increasingly, it is evident that this vital heterogeneity, which can maximize intellectual and material advancement, demands the overthrow of bourgeois-capitalism and bourgeois-ideology, due to the fact that "a free society... cannot be based on any particular creed"[16]. Namely, it cannot be based on the overarching domination of bourgeois-capitalism and bourgeois-ideology.

If all micro-narratives have equal claim to resources, because there is no overarching, universal, timeless truth and meta-narrative by which to judge, and if many active micro-narratives means maximum intellectual and material advancement, then, any individual claim to segments of private property, capital, knowledge, and money, as somehow rightfully belonging to a singular individual and/or any small oligarchical group, is moot, illegitimate, irrational, and fundamentally, counter-productive to intellectual and material advancement. If "there is no common measure"[17] by which to allocate resources, legitimately, justly, and fairly, and according to the post-modern anarchist point of view, there is no such common measure, then, every micro-narrative and individual has legitimate claim to the sum of socio-economic resources, in relative equal measure. Due to the fact, there is no underlying verity by which to deny resources for some and not others, and due to the fact that any unequal allocation of socio-economic resources impedes intellectual and material advancement.

Ultimately, all the bourgeois-capitalist canons, i.e., private property, individualism, hierarchy, greed and profiteering etc., are fictions, phantasms imposed upon society, illegitimately, both to impede collective development and truncate the general-population, namely, to keep it enslaved, both materially and intellectually, in confusion, delusion, nonsense and poverty, against its will and against its better nature. Since, its better nature is comprised of the fundamental concepts of egalitarianism, economic equality, collectivism and the sharing of resources, in relative equal measure.

In line with Jean-Francois Lyotard, the meta-narrative of bourgeois-capitalism is maintained, expanded, and traversed with terror, "the exercise of terror…[commanding all to] adapt your aspirations to our ends or else" [18]. Bourgeois-capitalism is totalitarian in nature; "it is unjust… [its] majority does not mean large number, it means great fear"[19], fear in all its forms, such as "imprisonment, unemployment, repression, hunger, anything you want"[20] in the sense that the meta-narrative of bourgeois-capitalism "does not respect…plurality"[21], but only its own myopic unity. As a result, any bourgeois-institution, or dominance hierarchy, which disseminates, endorses and/or promotes, individualism, capitalism, hierarchy, selfishness, private property and ironclad unity, is fundamentally anti-advancement, and in fact, willingly, participates in impeding intellectual and material advancement, i.e., the betterment of the human species as a whole.

In consequence, all bourgeois-institutions, or dominance hierarchies, should be utterly demolished, destroyed and/or abolished, on the valid and legitimate premise that these bourgeois-institutions and dominance hierarchies impeded intellectual and material advancement for the greatest number, by limiting access to socio-economic resources for the greatest number. That is, by the very fact that these bourgeois-institutions, deny, stifle, and impede, intellectual and material advancement and all rightful just claims, made by the multiplicity of micro-narratives in instituting radical collectivism, radical egalitarianism, and radical equality for all, including, the equal distribution of socio-economic resources.

The objective of post-modernism, or anarchism, is ultimately to reconstruct all the outdated, senile, bourgeois-institutions along collectivist, decentralist, horizontalist, and anti-capitalist lines of organization. Based on the fact that because there are no legitimate meta-narratives and/or universal truth-claims, any bourgeois-institution, or dominance hierarchy, which states otherwise and acts otherwise, is in actuality working against societal advancement and the validity of the democratic multiplicity of micro-narratives. These outdated, senile, bourgeois-institutions and dominance hierarchies are impeding socio-economic and intellectual development. These anti-advancement bourgeois-institutions and dominance hierarchies are impeding development, because, they are working against and in contradiction of plurality, equality and the valid demolition of all meta-narratives. That is, the basic fact that progress and "knowledge need a plurality of ideas" [22] in order to achieve maximum penetration and scientific development. The overthrow of the meta-narrative of bourgeois-capitalism means both progress and the redistribution of socio-economic resources for all, in relative equal measure.

Therefore, these senile, bourgeois-institutions and dominance hierarchies are categorically ripe for pragmatic demolitionism, namely, a type of material and conceptual demolition, which is valid on the post-modern premise that there are no acceptable valid reason, or argument, for the promotion of individual private-ownership, individual property, individual wealth, and financial inequality. The basis for pragmatic demolitionism is anarchist post-modernism. Namely, the fact that all bourgeois-capitalist principles impede the intellectual and material advancement of the human species by severely limiting plurality, autonomy and equality, i.e., the necessary plurality, autonomy and equality needed for maximum intellectual and material development.

Consequently, the rampant push for bourgeois-homogeneity and bourgeois-unity, we see burgeoning in and across western bourgeois-capitalist societies, including, within bourgeois-institutions, bourgeois-media, bourgeois-law, bourgeois-politics, bourgeois-academia etc., is in effect, purging all domains of variation, difference, and alternative viewpoints, which, according to Paul Feyerabend, "is to be expect in [bourgeois] totalitarian surroundings"[23]. Such purges of variation, difference, and alternative viewpoints, in and across the senile institutions of bourgeois-state-capitalism are primarily perpetrated via terror, both psychological and real. Meaning, they are perpetrated by force, a force derived from an unstated bourgeois ultimatum, commanding, everyone "say [and] do this, or else you'll never speak [in this domain] again"[24].

This is violence. It is a form of violence enacted "by laws, by peer pressure and by financial machinations" [25] etc., which have gradually drained, stopped, and eliminated, plurality from the domains of decision-making-authority and positions of power. The effect of this is the impediment of intellectual and material advancement in the name of an outdated, senile, bourgeois-capitalist status quo, which is increasingly ossifying itself into hierarchical rigidity, drastic financial inequality and, overall, socio-economic stagnation.

As a result, any bourgeois-institution or bourgeois hierarchy, which is constructed and designed to propagate and maintain the outdated, senile, bourgeois-capitalist status quo, at the expense of intellectual and material advancement, should be radically demolished, dismantled and/or abolished, on the very basis that these bourgeois-institutions and dominance hierarchies prevent intellectual and material development. These bourgeois-institutions and dominance hierarchies should be demolished on the basis that they deny collectivism, egalitarianism and equality for all.

When the zenith of post-modernism and anarchism is reached, when, post-modernism becomes anarchism in action, and anarchism becomes post-modernism in thinking, bourgeois rules and bourgeois regulations will be smashed and broken into a million pieces. These rules and regulations will be smashed and broken into a million pieces on the premise that these bourgeois rules and bourgeois regulations impeded advancement by favoring private property, individualism, bourgeois hierarchy and bourgeois money over equality and plurality. In short, all bourgeois-institutions and all bourgeois hierarchies should be usurped, because, these bourgeois-institutions and bourgeois hierarchies are solely in place to sustain a divisive, out of date, state-finance-corporate-aristocracy at the expense of real socio-economic equality, plurality, and heterogeneity.

The basis for the anarchist and post-modernist project is the fact that "there is no ontology…[and] no [underlying] rules"[26] for the validation of universal judgments. Specifically, we have no basic universal guidelines to live by, thus, to limit decision-making-authority strictly to a small minority, comprised in a small, tightly-knit, state-finance-corporate-aristocracy, is detrimental to the survival of society and the advancement of the human species.

There is no legitimate reason for the bourgeois form of hierarchical organization. As Paul Feyerabend states, "language can be bent in many directions…[as] understanding does not depend on any particular set of rules" [27]; as a result, "a single…worldview is going too far"[28]. It is too far, because, the bourgeois form of hierarchical organization kills collectivism, egalitarianism, and accessibility to resources for the greatest number, which is, the basis for maximum intellectual and material advancement. The bourgeois form of hierarchical organization should be dismantled, demolished and abolished, beyond any ability to re-establish its rule, because, as Feyerabend states, "interesting possibilities are removed [when institutions] firmly [insist] on the status quo"[29], while, denying the existence of all viable progressive exceptions growing out of diversity, plurality and heterogeneity.

So, what does this mean? This means that all institutions, or dominance hierarchies, should be horizontally reconstructed so as to permit maximum participation in decision-making-authority, by as many micro-narratives and/or individuals as possible, since, "knowledge needs plurality"[30] in order to grow. As a result, bourgeois-politics, bourgeois-law, bourgeois-education, bourgeois-media etc., should be radically opened-up to radical plurality, radical equality and radical multiplicity, devoid of the meta-narrative of bourgeois-capitalism. Namely, the point is to permit a litany of point of views and collectives, each with an equal amount of decision-making-authority, unencumbered by rigid rules and bourgeois regulations, able to fashion and refashion rules, regulations and institutions, at will, depending on the situation. In effect, as Lyotard states, we can only "be just, case by case"[31], guided by the idea of maintaining maximum plurality, so that democracy, participation, and accessibility is fully dilated and spread over as many micro-narratives and individuals as is conceivably possible.

Therefore, this means ultimately that the bourgeois-state-apparatus should be abolished, dismantled, and pragmatically demolished, since, it only acknowledges, promotes, and positions, select members of the upper-echelons of bourgeois-capitalism within its hierarchies of decision-making-authority. Moreover, this means that bourgeois-law should be abolished, dismantled, and pragmatically demolished, since, bourgeois-law only cherishes bourgeois forms of existence, i.e., individualism, bourgeois-property, bourgeois-money, bourgeois-hierarchy, and bourgeois capital etc., at the expense of all the micro-narratives that traverse society.

Finally, this means bourgeois-education should be abolished, dismantled, and pragmatically demolished, because, bourgeois-education instructs and promotes bourgeois obedience, bourgeois consciousness and bourgeois hierarchy. All of which, impede intellectual and material advancement, by both reinforcing the bourgeois-capitalist status-quo and denying a slew of valid perspectives and points of views, which can develop new knowledges, new technologies and new solutions. As Feyerabend states, "humans cannot have complete knowledge. There are too many things, too many events, too many situations" [32]. As a result, any intellectual and material advancement of knowledge and life must permit the participation of "many different maps of reality"[33] within the institutions of decision-making-authority so as to maximize the most opportunities for advancement. And, all bourgeois-institutions and bourgeois-hierarchies, which runs contrary to this demand for plurality and equality are in violation of the primary imperative inherent in the human species, progress. That is, the innate biological imperative and drive, housed in the species, commanding, an "overall mastery and comprehension of phenomena"[34], as soon as possible.

For this reason, bourgeois-education and, in general, bourgeois-institutions need to be opened-up to variation, with many flexible rules and regulations, designed to maximize democracy, participation and accessibility. For bourgeois-education, this means flexible standards and criterias, pertaining to the completion of degrees and educational competences. In effect, the plurality of multi-varied individuals and micro-narratives must be allowed to enter and exit, at will, the post-bourgeois-capitalist-university, without any time-limits on degree completion. These multi-varied individuals and micro-narratives must be permitted to change and collage courses and educational disciplines, at will, in order to attain certification. The point is to maximize diversity, plurality and heterogeneity etc.

Nothing must impede intellectual and material development in the sense that, as Feyerabend states, "there are many ways of ordering the world" [35] and each must be given the opportunity to democratically participate in the intellectual and material advancement of society. Limiting accessibility and the allocation of socio-economic resources, in relative equal measure, for the greatest number, ultimately, limits opportunities, capabilities, and the possibilities for intellectual and material development.

In short, clinging to the bourgeois-capitalist way of life is increasingly clarifying the basic fact that this mode of existence is inhibiting intellectual and material advancement, because, it denies the contribution of the vast majority, who are forced to abide by the limited parameters set-up by bourgeois-hierarchy and the bourgeois-capitalist status quo, that is, the meta-narrative of bourgeois-capitalism.

For post-modernism and anarchism, the crux of intellectual and material advancement requires collectivism, egalitarianism and maximum accessibility for all, which is exactly what is being suppressed by the meta-narrative of bourgeois-capitalism. Maximum "liberty is [attained] only...when the power of the representatives [of bourgeois-state-capitalism] is suspended and given back to the represented, [i.e., the people]" [36]. Only then, are plurality, equality, and accessibility for all, capable of being fully realized, which includes the prospect for the maximum advancement of society.

All told, all standards and criteria must be made ultra flexible, ultra-adaptable, and ultra-democratic, so as to maximize open-participatory-democracy and decision-making-authority in and across a maximum number of individuals, living, existing, and accessing, the post-bourgeois-capitalist-university and, in general, all post-bourgeois-capitalist-institutions. The point of anarchist post-modernism is to accommodate the variability of people and narratives entering and living through the post-bourgeois-capitalist-university and, in general, post-bourgeois-capitalist-institutions, because, knowledge "is not one tradition, it is many" [37]. And, the maximization of accessibility by all sorts of different people and narratives will lead to the maximization of mastery and comprehension over phenomena. The point is to accommodate maximum variability, plurality, and participation, at all levels of the post-bourgeois-capitalist-university and, in general, post-bourgeois-capitalist-institutions, due to the fact that, in actuality, there are no "universal measures of excellence" [38]. As a result, the more points of views permitted to participate and engage in decision-making-authority, the more chances there are of intellectual and material advancement. The point is to facilitate, enable, and accelerate intellectual and material advancement, by removing as many barriers as possible to intellectual and material development, which invariably means, the overthrow of the meta-narrative of bourgeois-capitalism in the name of anarchist post-modernism.

In sum, bourgeois-capitalism, the last meta-narrative of the Enlightenment, and all its individual tenets, such as individualism, bourgeois-hierarchy etc., must be jettisoned and abandoned at all levels of human existence, at all levels of everyday life, and at all levels of education, law, politics, and institutions. Because, bourgeois-capitalism impedes intellectual and material advancement, by denying the conditions for maximum intellectual and material development. Namely, the tenets of collectivism, egalitarianism, and accessibility for all must be allowed to mature and attain their full potentials. Therefore, nothing bourgeois, or capitalist, must survive the consequences of anarchist post-modernism. Absolutely nothing! As bourgeois-capitalism must be reduced to its rightful place and returned to its true position, as just another narrative and way of life, among many. As Feyerabend states,

> No invention is ever made in isolation, and no idea is, therefore, completely without (abstract or empirical) support....then the step back [from unity into

> plurality] is a step forward,…away from the tyranny of tightly-knit, highly corroborated, [collusionary bourgeois-capitalist] systems. [39]

Such a move is a step-forward, a step towards scientific maximization, diversity, and equality, for the greatest number. It is a step-forward into an open-participatory-democracy, devoid of class-divisions, race-divisions, gender-divisions etc., in service of collectivism, egalitarianism, and maximum accessibility for the greatest number. Therefore, only when post-modernism attains its apex and becomes indistinguishable with anarchism will the last stains of the meta-narrative of bourgeois-capitalism be wiped clean, and all senile, bourgeois-institutions finally be transformed into post-modern anarchist egalitarian-institutions.

Only, when post-modernism becomes fully radicalized and fully in-sync with its inherent anarchism will the last remaining meta-narrative of bourgeois-capitalism dissolve and disappear. Only, then will the essence of post-modernity realize itself with maximum clarity, namely, that anarchism is post-modernism in active-form and post-modernism is anarchism in thought form. Only, then will the greatest number of people be free of the tyranny of bourgeois-unity and be "given [real] equal rights, equal access to education, and…[real] positions of power" [40]. Because, at the moment, post-modernism is incomplete, it is divorced from its motor force, anarchism. As a result, it constantly excavates. It excavates, deep, continually towards its nitty-gritty, i.e., anarchism, knowing all too well, its full-maturation lies in the balance, namely, radial plurality, radical equality, and the total demolition of bourgeois-capitalism, right now!

Endnotes:

[1] Jean-Francois Lyotard, *The Post-Modern Condition*, Trans. Geoff Bennington and Brian Massumi (Minneapolis: University of Minnesota Press, 1984) p. xxiv.

[2] Jean-Francois Lyotard and Jean-Loup Thebaud, *Just Gaming*, Trans. Wlad Godzich (Minneapolis: University of Minnesota Press, 1985) p. 16.

[3] Ibid, p. 9.

[4] Ibid, p. 14.

[5] Michel Luc Bellemare, *The Structural-Anarchism Manifesto*: (The Logic of Structural-Anarchism Versus The Logic of Capitalism), (Montréal: Blacksatin Publications Inc., 2016) p. 25.b).

[6] Jean-Francois Lyotard and Jean-Loup Thebaud, *Just Gaming*, Trans. Wlad Godzich (Minneapolis: University of Minnesota Press, 1985) p. 74.

[7] Ibid, p. 102.

[8] Jacques Derrida, *Of Grammatology*, Trans. Gayatri Spivak (Baltimore: Johns Hopkins University Press, 2016) p. 350.

[9] Jean-Francois Lyotard, *The Post-Modern Condition*, Trans. Geoff Bennington and Brian Massumi (Minneapolis: University of Minnesota Press, 1984) p. 37.

[10] Paul Feyerabend, *Against Method*. (London: Verso, 1975) p. 202.

[11] Ibid, p. 127.

[12] Ibid, p. 32.

[13] Ibid, p. 105.

[14] Jean-Francois Lyotard and Jean-Loup Thebaud, *Just Gaming*, Trans. Wlad Godzich (Minneapolis: University of Minnesota Press, 1985) p. 16.

[15] Ibid, p. 28.

[16] Paul Feyerabend, *Against Method.* (London: Verso, 1975) p. 238.

[17] Ibid, p. 132.

[18] Jean-Francois Lyotard and Jean-Loup Thebaud, *Just Gaming*, Trans. Wlad Godzich (Minneapolis: University of Minnesota Press, 1985) p. 50.

[19] Jean-Francois Lyotard, *The Post-Modern Condition*, Trans. Geoff Bennington and Brian Massumi (Minneapolis: University of Minnesota Press, 1984) p. 64.

[20] Jean-Francois Lyotard and Jean-Loup Thebaud, *Just Gaming*, Trans. Wlad Godzich (Minneapolis: University of Minnesota Press, 1985) p. 99.

[21] Ibid, p. 99.

[22] Ibid, p. 98.

[23] Paul Feyerabend, *Against Method.* (London: Verso, 1975) p. 138.

[24] Ibid, p. 138.

[25] Jean-Francois Lyotard, *The Post-Modern Condition*, Trans. Geoff Bennington and Brian Massumi (Minneapolis: University of Minnesota Press, 1984) p. 46.

[26] Paul Feyerabend, *Against Method.* (London: Verso, 1975) p. 195.

[27] Jean-Francois Lyotard and Jean-Loup Thebaud, *Just Gaming*, Trans. Wlad Godzich (Minneapolis: University of Minnesota Press, 1985) p. 65.

[28] Paul Feyerabend, *Against Method.* (London: Verso, 1975) p. 257.

[29] Ibid, p. 245. [30] Ibid, p. 132.

[31] Jean-Francois Lyotard and Jean-Loup Thebaud, *Just Gaming*, Trans. Wlad Godzich (Minneapolis: University of Minnesota Press, 1985) p. 53.

[32] Paul Feyerabend, *Against Method.* (London: Verso, 1975) p. 205.

[33] Ibid, p. 256.

[34] Michel Luc Bellemare, *Treatise On Nhilism*, (Montréal: Blacksatin Publications Inc., 2017) 5.g).

[35] Paul Feyerabend, *Against Method.* (London: Verso, 1975) p. 166.

[36] Jacques Derrida, *Of Grammatology*, Trans. Gayatri Spivak (Baltimore: Johns Hopkins University Press, 2016) p. 323.

[37] Paul Feyerabend, *Against Method.* (London: Verso, 1975) p. 242.

[38] Ibid, p. 223.

[39] Ibid, p. 116.

[40] Ibid, p. 238.

Ch.5:

The Post-Modern Project Is Not Complete!

(A Post-Modern, Anarchist Critique of Left/Right Accelerationism)

The post-modern project is not complete. The fundamental meta-narrative of bourgeois-capitalism continues to persist and bewitch a vast sum of humanity. The reason is that post-modernism is divorced from its motor force, anarchism. If the post-modern condition is defined by "an incredulity towards meta-narratives"[1], then, the meta-narrative of bourgeois-capitalism is the last great bastion of the Enlightenment and its two-faced ideal of human equality and civic emancipation. Indeed, the meta-narrative of bourgeois-capitalism, the crown-jewel of the Enlightenment, continues to prosper and enslave, both mentally and physically, the rational human spirit, with dreams of material and immaterial luxury, opulence, and egalitarian abundance, which as always, are items manufactured on material and conceptual exploitation, domination, and the immiseration of the global workforce/population.

The bastard children of the Enlightenment and its zeal for human preservation and emancipation, through an ever-confining set of iron-cage rational-mechanisms, are comprised of two factions, currently in fashion. The first faction includes the dark fascist nightmares of the current, right-wing, wave of dark Enlightenment, namely, those who yearn for a vast set of repressive-mechanisms, under some sort of fascist, corporate, dictatorship. Specifically, the dark Enlightenment factions want to re-establish old Enlightenment dichotomies, wherein, people are put in their place through coercion, if need be. More or less, the dark

Enlightenment is a devil's bargain in the sense that it is an exchange of freedom for self-preservation, i.e., safety, it is as Horkheimer and Adorno state, "the exchange of freedom for the pursuit of self-preservation"[2], where, the "technological rationale is the rationale of domination, itself"[3]. Dark Enlightenment proponents believe it is through hard-line-totalitarianism, by which, bourgeois-capitalism can best be maximized in order to achieve its fullest potential. As a result, according to the dark Enlightenment, all democratic "political opposites are [to be fused into] one [,where, there is an] enthusiastic obedience to the [totalitarian] rhythms of the iron-system,...[namely] the absolute power of capitalism"[4]. This is a corporate-fascist-state, devoid of democracy, where all dissenting voices, including the general-population as a whole, is "relentlessly forced into [a hard-line] uniformity"[5].

In contrast to the dark Enlightenment, the second faction of the Enlightenment, currently in fashion, includes the sly, cunning, left-wing, Techno-Utopians, masquerading communists, who yearn for a vast technocratic, luxury, communist society, which is founded on a stringent adherence to instrumental-rationality and old, Habermasian, liberal, Enlightenment ideals like the Utopian notion of universal consensus at the expense of dissenting voices. That is, "a future-oriented left guided by the goal of universal emancipation"[6] through rational consensus, knowing full-well that consensus is the politically correct term for totalitarian ideological homogeneity, devoid of perspectival differences.

Either/or, both factions are errors in judgment and the product of mythical, Enlightenment, nonsensical thinking, namely, "the retreat [of] Enlightenment into mythology"[7]. These two positions/factions merely repeat the nauseating circularity of the dialectic of Enlightenment, which

Horkheimer and Adorno outlined so well, whereupon, "today…[we are] accelerating the advance towards [a totally] administrated world…[which] condemns the [rational] spirit to increasing darkness"[8], left or right. As a result, both factions are mesmerized and trapped within the dialectic of Enlightenment and/or the meta-narrative of bourgeois-capitalism, which through accelerationism of various types and kinds, left or right, unwittingly, attempt to un-tether the Enlightenment meta-narrative of bourgeois-capitalism in order to realize its full disastrous potential via the full-implementation of radical, instrumental-rationality, devoid of safeguards and all limits.

The right-wing faction yearns to do away with the Enlightenment, i.e., democracy, while, magnifying social regimentation and the mechanisms of bourgeois-capitalism, manifesting a survival of the fittest, winner take all, set of socio-economic conditions, grounded in self-interest and instrumental-rationality. This is totalitarian-corporate-fascism. In contrast, the left-wing faction yearns to do away with bourgeois-capitalism, while, magnifying the rational mechanisms of Enlightenment, where "whatever does not conform to the rule of computation and utility is suspect"[9] and the "power [of ideological consensus is] the principle of all [societal] relations"[10]. This is a technocratic, totalitarian form of communism. That is, a totalitarian-utopian-socialism based on unhinged instrumental-rationality, namely, instrumental-rationality striving towards universal consensus so as to produce a high-tech technocratic, luxury, Utopian-type of Stalinism. A form of Stalinism, wherein, an ironclad universal consensus rules and dominates an ideological plurality and socio-economic minority, reduced to inconsequentiality, inequality and total submission.

Therefore, contrary to left or right Enlightenment accelerationism, the point is to do away with the

Enlightenment and bourgeois-capitalism, altogether, not to cling fanatically to one or the other. This calls for a third option, the most radical option, beyond left and right accelerationism in the sense that this third option must do away with the the Enlightenment meta-narrative of bourgeois-capitalism, combined, since, both are synonymous and reflect one another, specifically, instrumental domination. As a result, the point of this philosophical essay is to outline this third revolutionary option in contrast to left/right accelerationism. The point is not to accelerate bourgeois-capitalism, either from the left or the right, including its mechanisms of exploitation and domination, praying that some exit strategy and/or event-horizon will present itself, wherein, bourgeois-capitalism will burst into flames, via its exploitative devices and/or morph into a corporate capitalist dictatorship, like Singapore and/or Techno-Utopian-Stalinism like Capitalist-Communist China. In contrast, the point is ultimately to override both bourgeois-capitalism and the Enlightenment, not to accelerate them until they break apart of their own accord. There is no guarantee that such a fatality will transpire through socio-economic acceleration.

The truth of the matter is both left/right accelerationists, forgo the revolution, and posit the responsibility of radical social change upon bourgeois-capitalist machinery, whether, this is Artificial Intelligence, or some other, technocratic mambo-jumbo. Both, posit revolutionary agency within capitalist machinery, rather than, within human agency, i.e., workers getting together to dispose of bourgeois-capitalism and the Enlightenment. As a result, both left/right accelerationists express the epitome of capitalist fetishism and Enlightenment myth-making, which is mistakenly attributed to machinery, where, as Marx states, "the products of human industry…and the power of knowledge [mistakenly appear as] the development of fixed capital [i.e. machinery]"[11] rather than human consciousness and human activity, from which any technological machinery actually springs from.

Consequently, the point is to subdue the grand-narratives of bourgeois-capitalism and the Enlightenment in order to blast them in unison to the periphery of socio-economic existence. The point is not "only to interpret the world, in various ways; the point…is to change it"[12]. As David Harvey correctly states, "capitalism will never fall on its own, it will have to be pushed. The accumulation of capital will never cease, it will have to be stopped"[13], meaning, no matter how much bourgeois-capitalism is accelerated it will never malfunction as leftist accelerationists argue. Technology will not lead to the systemic breakdown of bourgeois-capitalism.

However, through the acceleration of its socio-economic processes, bourgeois-capitalism may very well turn into a corporate fascist dictatorship as rightist accelerationists argue, due to the fact that unlimited speed, given that bourgeois-capitalism will not break-up of its own accord, will only intensify capitalist exploitation and domination. The result will be utterly horrific insofar as there will no longer be any institutional limits on the accumulation and extraction of surplus value, i.e., profits.

The same diagnostic applies, for the Enlightenment, it will not detonate sky-high on its own, it will have to be abolished, outright, in the name of a multi-level, poly-rationality founded on equality and diversity. Any notion that the Enlightenment can be rehabilitated and perfected, with or without bourgeois-capitalism, is utter delusion in the sense that the "Enlightenment is [inherently] totalitarian"[14], due to the fact that the "Enlightenment behaves toward things as a dictator toward men…in so far as [it] manipulate them"[15], according to its own mercenary, instrumental objectives.

Consequently, right-wing and left-wing accelerationism inevitably lead to forms of totalitarianism. Therefore, it is naïve of left/right accelerationists to think that totalitarianism could ever be more productive, more safe, and more stable, than bourgeois-state-capitalism, since, any faith in the reductive powers of instrumental-rationality is the "reversion of ... civilization to barbarism"[16], whether, this is a totalitarian corporate-fascist-state or a totalitarian-socialist-state.

Accelerationism, both coming from the left and the right, is mythical Enlightenment nonsense, whereupon, as Horkheimer and Adorno state, "thinking objectifies itself to become an automatic, self-activating process; an impersonation of the machine"[17]. It is the reduction of humans to inert mechanical processes and binary digits. It is the fetishism of machinery elevated to the point where "the [rational] spirit becomes the very apparatus of domination"[18]. As long as faith in the Enlightenment persists, any type of accelerationism leads to totalitarianism, totalitarian-socialism from the left and/or totalitarian-corporate-fascism from the right. Either/or, both left and right accelerationism results in the despotic enslavement of millions, despite the fact that "the Enlightenment [which] has always aimed at the liberating men from fear and establishing their sovereignty... the fully enlightened earth [inevitably] radiates disaster triumphant"[19]. Therefore, whether from the left and/or the right of the political-economic-spectrum, unless, the Enlightenment meta-narratives of bourgeois-capitalism is jettisoned, maximum autonomy, equality and a certain level of socio-economic stability will never be effectively achieved. It will not be achieved due to the fact that instrumental-rationality reduces the world and human existence to "total schematization"[20] as "the essence of Enlightenment [is]... domination"[21]. As a result, it is fools thinking, by left accelerationists, to think that one can do away with bourgeois-capitalism, while, staying true to Enlightenment ideals, avoiding any descent into communist totalitarianism. Because, as Horkheimer and Adorno state, totalitarianism is an inherent component of the Enlightenment and its ideals, including the meta-narrative of bourgeois-capitalism. Similarly, it is fools thinking, by the right accelerationists, to think that one can do away with the Enlightenment, while, staying true to bourgeois-capitalism, since, this almost certainly hastens a descent into hard-line totalitarianism.

In effect, left and right accelerationisms are two sides of the same Enlightenment coin, two-sides enacting the meta-narrative of bourgeois-capitalism, the crown-jewel of the dialectic of the Enlightenment, from two opposing, inherent, polarities of the Enlightenment. One is pitching the bright-side of Enlightenment ideals, without bourgeois-capitalism, side-stepping the Enlightenment nightmares of the 20th century, specifically, totalitarian-socialism and totalitarian-communism. And, the other is pitching the dark-side of the Enlightenment ideals, expressing a death-wish for totalitarian corporate-fascism in order to engender total safety, total stability, and the total reduction of humanity to calculability, i.e., where "formal logic… provides the Enlightenment…with the schema [for] the calculability of the world…[upon which] number is the [ultimate] canon"[22]. Either/or, both lead to despotism and domination, totalitarian-fascism and/or totalitarian-communism. Both left/right accelerationism is deception and trickery. Systematic nonsense designed to further the meta-narrative of Enlightenment and, by de-facto, traditional, bourgeois-capitalist myths, through a dialectic of Enlightenment, which "with every step becomes more deeply engulfed in mythology"[23], via, the tit-for-tat, spinning oscillation, inherent in this left/right Enlightenment dialectic.

The point is to dispose of all this, both the meta-narrative of Enlightenment and its meta-narrative of bourgeois-capitalism, so as not to encourage and further such meta-narratives in new fashionable disguises, which left and right accelerationism does.

Therefore, the post-modern project is not complete. It is not "un fait accompli". Because, the post-modern project has not reached its revolutionary zenith by fusing, conceptually and materially, with its motor force, anarchism. As a result, the Enlightenment meta-narrative of bourgeois-capitalism persists, unchallenged. It has not been disassembled, thus, it continues to dominate and exploit the sum of human existence, in various forms and formats, like the form and format of left/right accelerationism.

It is imperative that humans jettison the Enlightenment and its meta-narratives, especially, the meta-narrative of bourgeois-capitalism, which continue to fester both in right-wing and in left-wing styles of Enlightenment thinking. In sum, people must embrace the true revolutionary option, outside the Enlightenment and the meta-narrative of bourgeois-capitalism, due to the fact that this third revolutionary option is the one which actually leads out of the conceptual and material iron cage of the Enlightenment and its degenerate, bourgeois-capitalist offspring.

This third revolutionary option, which first reared its head with the advent of post-modernity and its mild incredulity towards meta-narratives, is a form of radical post-modernity, beyond post-modernism. It is anarchist post-modernity, that is, post-modern anarchism. This third revolutionary option is the re-invigoration of the mild, traditional post-modern, incredulity towards meta-narrative, in its most avant-garde and poignant form as an incessant onslaught of intellectual and material critique. It is anarchist post-modernism, or post-modern anarchism. It is the mild incredulity towards meta-narratives pushed to its Nth degree. It is a radical, revolutionary, incredulity towards meta-narratives of all kinds, with a special focus on the overthrow of the Enlightenment meta-narrative of bourgeois-capitalism, which includes all their sly strains of thought, which spawn from the fanaticism for profit and the fanaticism for total instrumentality:

> The Enlightenment promised the ideal that as people became more educated they would become more civilized and democratic. This has been shattered in the sense that as people have become more educated, they have become more suspect in relation to the workings of bourgeois-state-capitalism, the ruling, micro-fascist, oligarchical networks, and most importantly, their own neighbors. The reason is a strict emphasis on instrumental-rationality. As a result, humans have become more and more subject to domination and discipline, both by bourgeois-state-capitalism and their fellow citizens. In sum, the Enlightenment is totalitarian despotism and domination, par excellence. [Moreover] capitalist exploitation and domination has gone global and increasingly subjugates the micro-recesses of everyday life. Wherefore, the military-industrial-complex is now a totalitarian socio-economic formation, instrumentally engineered to maintain financial inequality, corporate feudalism, and the ruling, micro-fascist, oligarchical networks, i.e., the capitalist status quo, indefinitely. [24]

Indeed, the Enlightenment and bourgeois-capitalism, initially wanted the liberation of the rational human spirit, through a stern focus on instrumental-rationality, but instead, this has led increasingly into capitalist domination and enslavement, pertaining to the profit-making imperative of bourgeois-capitalism and the functionalist imperative of the Enlightenment.

The result is an ever-increasing rational subjugation of humanity by bourgeois-capitalism and the Enlightenment through such Machiavellian cults as left/right accelerationism. Left/right accelerationism is a symptom and/or a by-product of the dialectic of Enlightenment, i.e., the Enlightenment meta-narrative of bourgeois-capitalism. Left and right accelerationisms reflect Enlightenment mythology in different guises and both yearn to realize forms of totalitarianism derive from the two-sided polarity of the dialectic of Enlightenment.

For this reason, the post-modern project is not over as it has yet to reach its real revolutionary zenith through anarchism, whereupon, even the meta-ideals of bourgeois-capitalism and the Enlightenment, shall be overthrown in the name of real plurality, equality and heterogeneity, namely, classless, socio-economic heterogeneity. That is, an open-participatory patchwork/federation founded on basic financial guarantees for all, including the elimination of financial inequality, corporate feudalism and capitalist hierarchy. That is, the elimination of instrumental-rationality as the foundation-stone for any socio-economic formation, left or right. The objective is poly-rationality, i.e., a multi-dimensional, heterogeneous logic, which establishes a form of pragmatic-egalitarianism between a multiplicity of micro-narratives, sharing power equally. The aim is to install a post-Enlightenment, post-capitalist, multi-level, post-modern anarchism, capable of stimulating multi-dimensional, open-ended, socio-economic organizations, which maximize autonomy, equality, and positive, political-economic differences.

What the left/right accelerationists fail to understand is that machinery embodies, reflects, and functions, according to the ruling ideology, i.e., meta-narrative, which brought this machinery to life. The ruling set of narratives, or meta-narrative, give machinery purpose, meaning and value. This ruling set of narratives guide technology and technological-evolution, along certain parameters and lines of thought, limiting technological understanding and the human imagination to certain preconceived logical conclusions. That is, conclusions engineered via the ruling meta-narrative, which limit long-term, technological-evolution, due to a certain, reductive, parameters and homogeneous norms. As a result, according to Horkheimer and Adorno, there is a "stunting of …the imagination…[wherefore] no scope is left for the imagination"[25], other than, the reductive limiting scope sanctioned and established, by the ruling meta-narrative. This is the case with the instrumental-rationality of bourgeois-capitalism and the Enlightenment, namely, the Enlightenment meta-narrative of bourgeois-capitalism.

The Enlightenment and its bourgeois-capitalist meta-narrative limit and curtail progress by severely limiting options for intellectual and material development. Indeed,

> ideational comprehensive frameworks, [i.e.,ideologies/narratives] are the logics by which humans and things function and operate; they guide them, inform them, stimulate them, and make them move in all sorts of ways and fashions, both conceptually and materially etc., since, ideational comprehensive frameworks are the logics by which humans and things acquire method, meaning and purpose.[26]

Different narratives produce different technologies, with different characteristics and objectives. Different narratives produce different socio-economic parameters, inside different societies, resulting in different logical conclusions and technological developments. As a result, poly-rationality, in contrast to instrumental-rationality, is not reductive. It does not reduced or condensed everything to strict, scientific, instrumental, quantification. Hence, the poly-rationality of anarchist post-modernism can actually dissolve the Enlightenment meta-narrative of bourgeois-capitalism, while, establishing a vast, multi-dimensional, patchwork/federation of micro-narratives, devoid of any overarching meta-narrative. This multiplicity of micro-narratives is to be stitched loosely together, like patchwork, via a new post-Enlightenment, post-capitalist logic, i.e., the logic of anarchist post-modernism, structural-anarchism, namely, poly-rationality. As a result, bourgeois-capitalism, being the ruling, meta-narrative, for the last 250 years, ruling in concert with the instrumental-rationality of the Enlightenment, has meant that any machinery reflects, obeys, and functions, according to the Enlightenment meta-narrative of bourgeois-capitalism. The result of this is the suppression of logical options, analysis, and human imagination according to certain predetermined parameters and conclusions, concerning the future of society and the future of machine technological-evolution. It is in this regard that the Enlightenment meta-narrative of bourgeois-capitalism impedes technological options and developments by stifling human capacities and human imagination.

Unless people completely jettison the meta-narrative of the Enlightenment, especially bourgeois-capitalism, and embrace a radical incredulity towards all meta-narratives, specific to anarchism and radical post-modernism, people cannot escape bourgeois-capitalism and, by default, the

Enlightenment, no matter how fast and accelerated things are and/or get. The reason is the fact the "Enlightenment [has] always been a tool for the great manipulators of government"[27], whereupon, in the end, Enlightenment ideals for "the liberation of forces, universal freedom [and] self-determination"[28], ultimately, turn into conceptual enslavement and material domination. That is, bourgeois-capitalism and the Enlightenment become a "wholesale deception of the masses"[29].

The point is not to accelerate capitalist machinery, as left/right accelerationists would have us do. The point is not to intensify the meta-narrative of bourgeois-capitalism at the center of capitalist machinery, by somehow thinking that the acceleration of capitalist technology will bring forth new social relations and/or a new mode of production, through the downfall of bourgeois-capitalism or the Enlightenment. In the end, the logic of bourgeois-capitalism is set in stone, i.e., "to maximize profit, by any means necessary, at the lowest financial cost, as soon as possible"[30]; thus, bourgeois-capitalism thrives on speed and acceleration in the sense that its inherent nature is to attain an ultimate level of unregulated, unfettered-ness, as soon as possible, devoid of any considerations about the well-being of workforce/population. As a result,

> capitalism unfettered and unbound strives for an ironclad…military-industrial-complex, that is, a form of socio-economic organization where control, surveillance and work in the service of surplus value extraction and accumulation is paramount, highly functionalist, highly technocratic and highly regimented. [31]

Subsequently, bourgeois-capitalism does not need acceleration, since, its inherent instrumental-rationality and make-up is about acceleration.

Moreover, this fundamental fact about bourgeois-capitalism means that the logic of capitalism has no escape velocity. It has no exits, unless its intrinsic, exploitative logic, i.e., instrumental-rationality, is detonated sky-high, inside its own repressive parameters, which are, themselves, fused with the ideals of the Enlightenment.

Accelerating the logic of bourgeois-capitalism, as the left/right accelerationists demand, accelerates in turn capitalist exploitation, capitalist domination and capitalist immiseration to new heightened levels and new degrading humiliations. This is the essence of instrumental-rationality, the complete systematization of humans and the world, without options, without differences, without any social change, perfectly stratified and perfectly hierarchized, according to the underlying ideals and logic of the Enlightenment and bourgeois-capitalism.

Therefore, left/right accelerationists play into the hands of the Enlightenment meta-narrative of bourgeois-capitalism, when, they demand socio-economic acceleration. In effect, they fuel ever-increasing repression and deeper encroachments by the meta-narrative of bourgeois-capitalism into everyday life, when, they demand speed and acceleration. As Horkheimer and Adorno state, "the technical and social tendencies [of the Enlightenment and bourgeois-capitalism], always interwoven, [forever] converge in the total schematization of men"[32]. There is no escaping this fact. Consequently, both bourgeois-capitalism and the Enlightenment must be done away with, together. Not one, or the other, but, both must be done away with. This is apex and the revolutionary zenith of the post-modern anarchist project, namely, anarchist post-modernism.

The Enlightenment and the logic of bourgeois-capitalism give birth to many mechanical variations of themselves, their offspring wear many different masks, but, underneath their seeming Enlightened natures, that is, instrumental-rationality, the same old bourgeois-capitalism permeates, i.e., "to maximize profit, by any means necessary, at the lowest financial cost, as soon as possible"[33]. The reason is that the Enlightenment and

> the logic of capitalism [are]… totalitarian [meta]-languages that design copies of [themselves], ad infinitum, a vast array of ideological facsimiles, both material and conceptual, which disseminate the logic of capitalism [and the Enlightenment] in various concealed and unconcealed forms.[34]

Left/right accelerationisms are examples of this fact. Left and right accelerationisms are cunning facsimiles of bourgeois-capitalism and the Enlightenment, which beneath their fashionable calls for ultimate speed, only perpetuates the logical imperatives of bourgeois-capitalism and the Enlightenment in different disguises.

As a result, left and right accelerationism are the bastard children of the meta-narrative of bourgeois-capitalism and the Enlightenment. In fact, it is the Enlightenment meta-narrative of bourgeois-capitalism, itself, which brings forth, out of totalitarian, instrumental-rationality, this army of pseudo-revolutionaries, pseudo-luminaries, and pseudo-tech-gurus, both on the left and the right, in an effort to expand its despotism and its dominion over society. As a result, this army of pseudo-revolutionaries, pseudo-luminaries, and pseudo-tech-gurus, are instrumentally designed to perpetuate the meta-narrative of capitalism, the crown-jewel of the Enlightenment, in various new forms and up-to-date styles, so as to maximize human subjugation and the accumulation and extraction of surplus value, i.e., capitalist profit. Once again, the cost for all these counterfeits falls unto the workforce/population, who, as always, pay through the nose with their blood and sweat.

Post-capitalism in the accelerationist mode is unattainable, and will come to relatively nothing, if it solely consists in accelerating the logic, the machinery and the mechanisms of bourgeois-capitalism to the Nth degree, without any fundamental call for total revolution. And, moreover, post-capitalism in the accelerationist mode is unattainable, and will come to relatively nothing, if it insists on remaining under the umbrella of instrumental-rationality, i.e., the Enlightenment. Reanimating the Enlightenment in any shape and/or form, whether, as a totalitarian fascist nightmare or as a totalitarian-communist techno-dystopia, plays into the hands of the Enlightenment meta-narrative of bourgeois-capitalism, furthering its inherent "nihilistic anti-life force"[35].

The Enlightenment and its socio-economic meta-narrative of bourgeois-capitalism are totalitarian and tend towards despotism, "economic coercion and the freedom to choose what is always [ideologically] the same"[36]. From the left and/or the right, there is no escape velocity from this basic fact. Unless people jettison the Enlightenment meta-narrative of bourgeois-capitalism, and embrace a radical, post-modern, anarchist, incredulity towards all meta-narratives, specifically, bourgeois-capitalism and the Enlightenment, all is lost.

All is lost, because, as Horkheimer and Adorno state, "the irrationalism of totalitarian capitalism [and the Enlightenment], whose way of satisfying [human] needs has an objectified form [determined] by domination, makes the satisfaction of [human] needs [all but] impossible.[Since, both] tend towards the extermination of mankind"[37]. As a result, to accelerate this logic of domination and enslavement to the Nth degree, as left/right accelerationists want, is lunacy, a lunacy, reeking of bourgeois-capitalist opportunism and social irresponsibility, a crime against humanity.

In reality, the only exit strategy, out of bourgeois-capitalism and the Enlightenment is the pragmatic-application of the post-modern anarchist incredulity towards meta-narratives to the last standing meta-narratives of the Enlightenment, bourgeois-capitalism. And, this includes all the degenerate offshoots of the Enlightenment and bourgeois-capitalism curled-up on both sides of the accelerationist debate. The post-modern revolution is an anarchist revolution, founded on multi-varied, poly-rationality, without meta-narrative, without left/right accelerationism, without bourgeois-capitalism, and without the Enlightenment. The post-modern anarchist revolution is a radical form of anarchist post-modernity inherently anti-Enlightenment, anti-bourgeois and anti-capitalist, in nature.

The post-modern anarchist revolution is an attempt to rid civilization of the cunning instrumental horrors of bourgeois-capitalism and the Enlightenment. As a result, the end of instrumental-rationality cannot transpire on any meth-speed form of accelerationism, that is, any fantastic injection of technocratic meth-amphetamines etc., as

> real history is the unfolding of the will to power, a convergence of mental and physical forces and/or logics, pitted against one another in a multiplicity of fluctuating, antagonistic and/or mutual-aid relationships, vying for contextual supremacy. Real history is a fiery molten crucible, anarchy, buried deep, beneath manufactured pseudo-history and superficiality, ever-ready to explode, unfold, by way

> of the revolutionary rabble. Purged and purified of capitalist modes and relations, real history will glisten, glisten through a new logical apparatus and paradigm. And, any small impetus can germinate and activate the people's revolution. So, make haste… rabble-rouser, grab history, own it, and bend it to your will, less history slips between your fingers into something other, something false, something that will wield real history against you from above.[38]

Real history, real radical social change, germinates deep within the artificial parameters of bourgeois-capitalism and the Enlightenment. It germinates in the hearts and minds of the workforce/population, consciously and unconsciously, and nowhere else. Radical social change is always post-modern and anarchist in form and in agency.

Ultimately, radical social change does not reside in the titanium body of any capitalist machinery as accelerationists would have us believe. All told, the post-modern project is not complete as it is not yet fully aware of its motor force, anarchism, but, everyday this is becoming less so. In sum, "the self-inflicted, global-suicide of totalitarian-capitalism lies behind the blazing eyes of millions marching, together, arm in arm over its cold metallic corpse, smashed to pieces, under the militant boot of structural-anarchism, commanding, *IMMEDIATE DEMOLITIONIST-ACTION AND GENERAL-STRIKE!"*[39].

Endnotes:

[1] Jean-Francois Lyotard, *The Post-Modern Condition*, Trans. Geoff Bennington and Brian Massumi (Minneapolis: University of Minnesota Press, 1984) p. xxiv.

[2] Max Horkheimer and Theodor Adorno, *Dialectic of Enlightenment*, Trans. John Cumming (New York: Continuum, 2000) p. 40.

[3] Ibid, p. 121.

[4] Ibid, p. 120.

[5] Ibid, p. 124.

[6] Nick Srnicek and Alex Williams, *Inventing The Future: Postcapitalism and a World Without Work*, (New York: Verso, 2015) p. 23.

[7] Max Horkheimer and Theodor Adorno, *Dialectic of Enlightenment*, Trans. John Cumming (New York: Continuum, 2000) p. xiv.

[8] Ibid, p. x-xiv.

[9] Ibid, p. 6.

[10] Ibid, p. 9.

[11] Karl Marx, *"Grundrisse", The Marx-Engels Reader*, ed. Robert C. Tucker (New York, New York: W.W. Norton & Company Inc., 1978) p. 285.

[12] Karl Marx, *"Theses on Feuerbach", The Marx-Engels Reader*, ed. Robert C. Tucker (New York, New York: W.W. Norton & Company Inc., 1978) p. 145.

[13] David Harvey, *The Enigma of Capital*, (Oxford, United-Kingdom: Oxford University Press, 2010) p. 260.

[14] Max Horkheimer and Theodor Adorno, *Dialectic of Enlightenment*, Trans. John Cumming (New York: Continuum, 2000) p. 6.

[15] Ibid, p. 9.

[16] Ibid, p. xvi.

[17] Ibid, p. 25.
[18] Ibid, p. 36.
[19] Ibid, p. 3.
[20] Ibid, p. 35.
[21] Ibid, p. 32.
[22] Ibid, p. 7.
[23] Ibid, p. 12.
[24] Michel Luc Bellemare, *The Structural-Anarchism Manifesto*: (The Logic of Structural-Anarchism Versus The Logic of Capitalism), (Montréal: Blacksatin Publications Inc., 2016) pp. 33.a) -33.b).
[25] Max Horkheimer and Theodor Adorno, *Dialectic of Enlightenment*, Trans. John Cumming (New York: Continuum, 2000) pp. 126-127.
[26] Michel Luc Bellemare, *The Structural-Anarchism Manifesto*: (The Logic of Structural-Anarchism Versus The Logic of Capitalism), (Montréal: Blacksatin Publications Inc., 2016) p. 15.d).
[27] Max Horkheimer and Theodor Adorno, *Dialectic of Enlightenment*, Trans. John Cumming (New York: Continuum, 2000) p. 44.
[28] Ibid, p. 93.
[29] Ibid, p. 42.
[30] Michel Luc Bellemare, *The Structural-Anarchism Manifesto*: (The Logic of Structural-Anarchism Versus The Logic of Capitalism), (Montréal: Blacksatin Publications Inc., 2016) p. 26.h).
[31] Ibid, p. 27.a).
[32] Max Horkheimer and Theodor Adorno, *Dialectic of Enlightenment*, Trans. John Cumming (New York: Continuum, 2000) p. 35.

[33] Michel Luc Bellemare, *The Structural-Anarchism Manifesto*: (The Logic of Structural-Anarchism Versus The Logic of Capitalism), (Montréal: Blacksatin Publications Inc., 2016) p. 42.b).

[34] Ibid, p. 17.b).

[35] Max Horkheimer and Theodor Adorno, *Dialectic of Enlightenment*, Trans. John Cumming (New York: Continuum, 2000) p. 44.

[36] Ibid, p.165-p. 167.

[37] Ibid, p. 55.

[38] Michel Luc Bellemare, *The Structural-Anarchism Manifesto*: (The Logic of Structural-Anarchism Versus The Logic of Capitalism), (Montréal: Blacksatin Publications Inc., 2016) p. 72.e).

[39] Ibid, p. 72.f).

PART TWO

Ch.6:

Why The Meta-Narrative of Bourgeois-Capitalism Must Be Completely And Utterly Demolished:

(The Case For Demolitionism)

I

The meta-narrative of bourgeois-capitalism is both hindering socio-economic development and stifling socio-economic heterogeneity in the sense that it continually perpetuates mediocrity and homogeneity, ad nauseam, in and across the stratums and upper-echelons of bourgeois-capitalism. Hence, why the meta-narrative of bourgeois-capitalism needs to be demolished and is demolishing, itself, of its own accord. The aim is to accelerate this destructive process via the full-onslaught of pragmatic demolitionism, that is, through an incessant material and conceptual critique of bourgeois-state-capitalism from the perspective and underlying principles of anarchist post modernism.

The fact is, any honest intellectual, looking at our society, today, can factually see that the best and brightest do not always, or if ever, occupy the upper-echelons of any contemporary dominance-hierarchy, academia, politics, business etc., in and across the stratums of bourgeois-capitalism. In actuality, today, the reverse is the case in the sense that we see constantly that the best and brightest are being left behind, or are forced to remain, on the lower-rungs of bourgeois-society, scrounging for their existence, while, the system favors and promotes an obedient herd-mediocrity at every level. That is, those individuals or groups who best subserviently, ideologically, and obediently, buttress and propagate, the bourgeois status-quo, namely, those towing, with a certain docile obedience, the dominant ideological tenets of bourgeois-capitalism, bourgeois-academia, bourgeois-elites, and the overall, bourgeois way of life. As a result, the meta-narrative of bourgeois-capitalism needs to be completely and utterly demolished because its goal is not progress and/or socio-economic development, its goal is socio-economic inertia, creative stagnation and social immobility, which is the essence of its continued governance over the global-population. Real change is the anti-thesis to the continued supremacy of the meta-narrative of bourgeois-capitalism.

According to Nietzsche, in and across western civilizations and western cultures, it is always the most mediocre of our species, which are the most apt to succeed in reaching the top of any bourgeois-capitalist dominance-hierarchy, because, these herd-animals embody and represent the most enduring, conservative, and brutish, characteristics of our species, i.e., the inhuman and the average. There propensity for the inhuman and the average gives these mediocre individuals an advantage over more evolved and civilized individuals, who have broader considerations and respect for differences and others.

Ultimately, their limited vocabularies and truncated intellects give these herd-animals an advantage over more evolved individuals, by unburdening their conscience of ethical considerations, moral dilemmas, and any sort of thoughtfulness. Essentially, their advantage lies in the fact that they have reduced the world to black and white, right and wrong etc., thus, giving themselves an advantage over more thoughtful beings and considerate beings. To quote, Nietzsche, the advantage of herd-mediocrity is that "the mediocre are, like the herd, little troubled with [ethical] questions and conscience—[they are] cheerful"[1] and decisive in their behaviors. By being linguistically limited, these mediocre individuals are simultaneously intellectually limited, thus, lacking any lasting empathy for anything different and/or anything other. In effect, they are self-absorbed for the most part. As Nietzsche states, "in so far as the mass is dominant it bullies the exceptions…[it is a] resistance to higher types"[2]. The result is, for Nietzsche, under the meta-narrative of bourgeois-capitalism, humanity is ruled by "the herd, i.e., that…sum of zeros…[wherein] it is virtuous to be a zero"[3] in the sense that only zeros are permitted to climb the dominance-hierarchies of bourgeois-capitalism, due to their docile conservative natures.

In a nutshell, it is zeros who are most apt to climb the dominance-hierarchies, set-up by the meta-narrative of bourgeois-capitalism, due to the fact that stasis, immobility, and inertia, is the goal of the meta-narrative of bourgeois-capitalism. Zeros are all about conceptual and material stasis, immobility and inertia.

According to the meta-narrative of bourgeois-capitalism, the goal is stasis, immobility and inertia, because, these guarantee the authoritative contextual-supremacy of any ruling meta-narrative, specifically, the meta-narrative of bourgeois-capitalism. And, because average herd-mediocrity is the most static, immobile, and inert segment of the general-population, it is thus favored over anything that embodies, or might embody, exceptionalism and radical social change. This is the reason why the meta-narrative of bourgeois-capitalism promotes herd-mediocrity at every turn into the upper-echelons of its bureaucracy and, simultaneously, attacks, stifles, and asphyxiates, anything different, anything higher, which might upset lame bourgeois tastes, bourgeois-hierarchies and the overall bourgeois-capitalist status-quo.

Social development, social mobility, social equality and/or any form of creativity, are all detrimental to the long-term, staying-power of the meta-narrative of bourgeois-capitalism, thus, why the agents of the meta-narrative of bourgeois-capitalism hinder and stifle, both consciously and/or unconsciously, anything that runs-counter to the meta-narrative of bourgeois-capitalism. The point is to maintain the supremacy of bourgeois-capitalism, by any means necessary. Moreover, it is for this reason that the meta-narrative of bourgeois-capitalism must eventually be demolished via the full anarchist onslaught of pragmatic demolition, since, the meta-narrative of bourgeois-capitalism prevents development, namely, it prevents anything which embodies and reflects post-modernity, due to the fact that post-modernity represents radical equality, plurality and a rabid antipathy towards all meta-narratives.

According to Nietzsche, it is the job of the herdsmen of bourgeois-capitalism "to retain…the herd, flatter it, work with [it, in order to] consolidate its mediocrity"[4], and direct it against any exceptional narratives and/or Über-mensch. For Nietzsche, "it is the object of herd education [via the herdsmen] to create in the herd member…a definite faith concerning the nature of man" [5], wherefore, inertia, averageness, and the defence of the bourgeois status-quo are deemed the epitome of intelligence and good Christian citizenship.

Indeed, solidifying the bourgeois status-quo, by championing herd-mediocrity as the highest and most valuable attribute, in order to climb the bourgeois dominance hierarchy, is la raison d'être of bourgeois-education. The point of bourgeois-education consists in marshalling the vindictiveness embodied in herd-mediocrity against anything which is different, plural, and exceptional. Namely, all that is not generic, average, and a part of the bourgeois status-quo, must be eradicated from the capitalist-system. Anything which remotely reflects post-modernity, or anarchism, must be killed off. This is the goal of bourgeois-education, i.e., indoctrination, moderation, and the creation of a dictatorship of the center and the middle, whereupon, obedience is intelligence and intelligence is obedience. Anything else is worthless and expendable.

Behind the institutions of bourgeois-capitalism, according to Nietzsche, lies "three powers (1) the instinct of the herd against the...independent; (2) the instinct of the suffering and underprivileged against the fortunate; (3) the instinct of the mediocre against the exceptional"[6]. Subsequently, it is the herd and its mediocrity which reigns supreme beneath the meta-narrative umbrella of bourgeois-capitalism, nothing post-modern and/or anarcho-exceptional is given precedence over herd-mediocrity. And, due to this fact, social advancement, i.e., the full-brunt of post-modernism, has not been attained. Meaning, post-modernism has yet to achieve its zenith, its apex and/or its full-maturity, pragmatic-egalitarianism, namely, the egalitarian allotment of socio-economic resources among all citizens, in relative equal measure, giving unto Caesar what rightfully belongs unto Caesar, an anarchist society.

To the contrary, beneath the ruling meta-narrative of bourgeois-capitalism, the exceptional is continually reduced to insignificance, in-consequentiality, and irrelevance. The exceptional is constantly reduced to the lower-rungs of the bourgeois-capitalist dominance-hierarchies in favor of docile, obedient, herd-mediocrity, which in vast numbers increasingly occupy the upper-echelons of bourgeois-capitalism. The reason for this, Nietzsche states, is that "the herd feels the exception, whether it be below or above it, as something opposed and harmful to it"[7], while, for the meta-narrative of bourgeois-capitalism, herd-mediocrity is allotted continual precedence over the exceptional because herd-mediocrity insures its continued authority, longevity and supremacy.

Of course, the end result of this degenerate capitalist process is socio-economic inertia, creative stagnation, and nihilism, that is, an "inner decay and disintegration… [wherefore] nothing stands firmly on its feet [anymore]"[8], but is at the mercy of the overwhelming force of herd-mediocrity. Namely, an overwhelming mediocrity that dictates socio-historical unfolding via a totalitarian "community spirit [and] the [nationalist] fatherland"[9]. Ultimately, crisis ensues. And, crisis opens the door to radical social change, that is, certain forms of change that weaken the ruling meta-narratives and in contrast stimulate socio-economic transformations, i.e., anarchism and post-modernism.

II

According to Thomas Kuhn, revolutions and insurrections are prickly affairs, which tend to begin with the failure of existing dominant rules, meaning, the "failure of existing rules is the prelude to a search for new ones"[10]. For Kuhn, an initial crisis in the existing rules presents a possible break, which may lead to a revolution and insurrection in favor of new rules, institutions and, ultimately, a paradigm-shift. In effect, a crisis opens the door to radical social change, if that door is not soon closed. Left open for an extended period of time, radical social change is inevitable, due to the crisis. As Kuhn States,

> revolutions are inaugurated by a growing sense, often restricted to a segment of the…community, that existing institutions have ceased to adequately to meet the problems posed by an environment that they have in part created. The sense of malfunction that...lead to crisis is [a] prerequisite to revolution. Revolutions aim

> to change…institutions in ways that those institutions themselves prohibit.[11]

During the initial stages, according to Kuhn, "increasing numbers of individuals become increasingly estranged from political life and behave more and more eccentrically within it"[12], eventually, this estrangement prompts these individuals to "commit themselves to some concrete proposal for the reconstruction of society in a new institutional framework"[13]. Sooner or later, if the crisis is not resolves through the current institutional framework, "society…[divides] into competing camps or parties, one seeking to defend the old institutional constellation, the others seeking to institute new ones"[14]. When this binary bifurcation has occurred, revolution and insurrection is assured, due to the fact that all "political recourse fails"[15]. According to Kuhn, it fails because the two camps

> differ about the institutional matrix within which…change is to be achieved and evaluated. [In effect,] they acknowledge no supra-institutional framework for the adjudication of revolutionary difference, the parties to [such] a revolutionary conflict must finally resort to the techniques of mass persuasion, often including force. [Because] the choice [in the final analysis is] between competing institutions, …a choice between incompatible modes of community life. [16]

These incompatible modes of community life aggravate the revolution and insurrection, stimulating the advent of a new paradigm and the dissolution of the old paradigm, i.e., meta-narrative, or vice versa, the result is the dissolution of the new paradigm and the maintenance of the old paradigm, i.e., meta-narrative. In the end, conflict and propaganda decides the outcome.

Notwithstanding, ultimately, it is the senility of a meta-narrative, i.e., paradigm, which leads to revolution and insurrection, that is, radical social change, either for, or against, the burgeoning new micro-narratives. And, specifically, the meta-narrative of bourgeois-capitalism is fast approaching this precipice. That is, "a relatively sudden and unstructured event like a gestalt-switch"[17], which changes everything, where, as Kuhn states, with the "paradigm [,i.e., meta-narrative] change, the world itself [also] changes"[18], whereupon, nothing is left unchanged. Consequently, it is the slow rising inertia of the meta-narrative of bourgeois-capitalism, brought about by its fanatic celebration and propagation of herd-mediocrity, which is, propelling the meta-narrative of bourgeois-capitalism towards sudden revolution, insurrection, demolition, and its own obsolescence. The reason being the fact, the meta-narrative of bourgeois-capitalism refuses to yield to the coming apex of anarchist post-modernism, which demands the dissolution of all meta-narratives in favor of narrative egalitarianism. As a result, in contrast, the meta-narrative of bourgeois-capitalism is instead increasingly embracing stagnation, inertia, and immobility. It is increasingly manufacturing herd-mediocrity. It is increasingly manufacturing herd-mediocrity in increasingly higher and higher dosages so as to freeze socio-economic development in its tracks, thus, preventing the full-maturation of post-modernism and anarchism. This degenerate process is slowly and gradually manufacturing a powder-keg full of social dynamite, soon to explode at the sudden flick of a switch, namely, a gestalt-switch.

Specifically, the meta-narrative of bourgeois-capitalism refuses to yield to the zenith and apex of post-modernity, i.e., an anarchist institutional framework of pragmatic-egalitarianism, whereupon, all micro-narratives share the sum of socio-economic resources, in relative equal measure, devoid of any overarching meta-narrative. As a result, bourgeois-capitalism sees post-modernism and anarchism as its anti-thesis, an anti-thesis geared towards its ultimate demise, due to the fact, post-modernism and anarchism embody a radical antipathy towards meta-narratives, including the meta-narrative of bourgeois-capitalism. Because of this, anarchist post-modern antipathy towards bourgeois-capitalism, as Kuhn states, any "transition [to a new paradigm]…cannot be made a step at a time, forced by logic and neutral experience. Like the gestalt-switch, it must occur all at once (though not necessarily in an instant) or not at all."[19], the reason being the fact that the meta-narrative of bourgeois-capitalism will not go quietly into obsolescence.

In sum, bourgeois-capitalism will have to be pragmatically demolished, brick by brick, thrown forcefully into the dust-bin of history. And, as usual, the primary obstacle to radical social change is herd-mediocrity. That is, the herd-mediocrity manufactured by the meta-narrative of bourgeois-capitalism, which has been elevated beyond its capabilities, intellect, and wildest dreams into the upper-echelons of bourgeois-capitalism, preventing any smooth transition and/or development out of bourgeois-capitalism. Herd-mediocrity is what poses the most troublesome element for any paradigm-shift or gestalt-switch, since, embodied in the herd, gently placed there by the indoctrinating mechanisms of bourgeois-capitalism, lies" the tradition of [bourgeois] values"[20], holding the Enlightenment meta-narrative of bourgeois-capitalism firmly in place. Due to this, any transition out of the meta-narrative of bourgeois-capitalism must be a revolution and/or insurrection, namely, a relatively instantaneous gestalt-switch or nothing at all. Any transition out of bourgeois-capitalism must be an active conceptual and material demolition of bourgeois-capitalism.

Along a similar line of thought as Kuhn, for Marx, this gestalt-switch is the result of an incongruity and/or conflict between the forces of production and the relations of production embodied in a governing mode of production, whereupon, "the changes in the economic foundation lead sooner or later to the transformation of the whole immense superstructure"[21], including, the ruling paradigm and/or meta-narrative. According to Marx, a mode of production is a particular form of organization and equilibrium between certain forces of production and relations of production between human beings, reflecting a certain form of consciousness, which ultimately, determines the way resources are produced, distributed, and consumed, within a specific society. As Marx states,

> in the social production of their existence, men inevitably enter into definite relations, which are independent of their will, namely relations production appropriate to a given stage in the development of their material forces of production. The totality of these relations of production constitutes the economic structure of society, the real foundation, on which arises a legal and political superstructure and to which correspond definite forms of social consciousness. The mode of production of material life conditions the general process of social, political and intellectual life. At a certain stage of development, the material productive forces…come into conflict with the existing relations of production [wherefore]…the productive forces [and] these relations turn into … fetters. Then begins an era of social revolution…in which men become conscious of this conflict and fight

> it out. No social order is ever destroyed before all the productive forces for which it is sufficient have been developed, and new superior relations of production never replace older ones before the material conditions for their existence have matured within the framework of the old society.[22]

In effect, for Marx, a ruling mode of production structures the way a society functions, operates, and is organized. And, when a radical disconnect presents itself between the forces of production and the relations of production a conflict and crisis ensues, which in the end, if the conflict and crisis is substantial enough, results in the installation of a new mode of production and, in general, a new socio-economic formation and/or society.

However, what if a ruling mode of production and its adjacent form of consciousness also structures revolutionary paradigm-shifts, out of the very mode of production and ruling meta-narratives, which seek to prevent these shifts. Meaning, the gestalt-switch needed to transition into a new paradigm, or meta-narrative, is the product of friction and conflict between the forces of production and the relations of production, deep inside the ruling mode of production. The conversion experience Kuhn states is akin to a gestalt-switch is the result of a disequilibrium between the material forces of production and the ideological relations of production, both conceptual and material, transpiring deep within the economic base of society. In effect, the presence of a radical disconnect between the forces of production and relations of production manifests a conversion experience, i.e., a gestalt-switch, when these forces of production and these relations of production fall into conflict and a constant escalating crisis. It is then that individuals become aware that something is wrong and something must change, and begins to look for a new narrative, or paradigm, to better his or her situation. It is for this reason that Kuhn states

> the conversion experience…[is] a gestalt-switch…at the heart of the revolutionary process…[which] provides motives for conversion and a climate in which it is more likely to occur. [Crisis and conflict provide] points of entry for the neural reprogramming that… must underlie [the] conversion.[23]

For Marx, the nexus of any revolutionary process lies in production, the ruling mode of production stationed at the economic base of society. Therefore, this is where paradigm-shifts and the dissolution of meta-narratives are most likely to occur. However, because today the general-population is constantly immersed in a perpetual moment of production, revolutions can germinate from anywhere at any time. Subsequently, an escalation of a crisis and a conflict within the economic base and across the super-structure of society can spread like wild-fire, engulfing the sum of socio-economic existence.

In addition, with this tightly woven-integration of society, new superior sets of productive relations can germinate from anywhere at any time. That is, the advent of a new mode of production and a new set of micro-narratives, can reconfigure society unexpectedly according to new underlying principles and/or logic.

Moreover, demolitionism is a natural development brought about by the escalating crisis and conflict between the forces of production and relations of production, since, demolitionism is motivated by an increasing estrangement and disconnect between people and the forces of production. As a result, demolitionism increasingly detaches individuals from the ideological opiate of bourgeois-capitalism in and across the sum of social production. Acts of demolitionism essentially wake people from their bourgeois ideological slumber. In effect, they increasingly see the large disconnect between bourgeois-ideology and reality, namely, the increasing chasm that lies between their real existence and the ideals showered unto them by the meta-narrative of bourgeois-capitalism.

In fact, demolitionism increasingly leads the general-population towards paradigm-shift and a gestalt-switch, because, the conflict between the forces of production and relations of production is incessant. In effect, the general-population by itself begins to yearn and to demand, of its own accord, a new socio-economic-formation, i.e., a new mode of production, devoid of the meta-narrative of bourgeois-capitalism. It is the very friction, conflict, and crisis, manifested by the disconnect between the forces of production and the dominant relations of production, which produces disillusionment and the demolition-motive in the general-population, i.e., the motive for the total destruction of the meta-narrative of bourgeois-capitalism.

The point of demolitionism is to manifest a paradigm-shift and a gestalt-switch in order to alleviate the ever-increasing disillusionment and disconnect between the forces of production and relations of production. In essence, the point of demolitionism is to reduce all meta-narratives, back from which they came, the plethora of micro-narratives, so as to usher-in an era of post-modern anarchism, that is, total equality, autonomy and pragmatic-egalitarianism.

Of course, with any homogenizing, obdurate, fanatical ideology like the meta-narrative of bourgeois-capitalism, one does not win converts by resorting to good argument and sound logic, the meta-narrative of bourgeois-capitalism requires more than good argument and sound logic, if it is to step aside. In such extreme ideological situations, as Max

Planck put it, “truth does not triumph by convincing its opponents and making them see the light, but rather [triumphs] because its opponents eventually die”[24]. Therefore, demolitionism simply hastens the inevitable, the disintegration of the meta-narrative of bourgeois-capitalism.

Endnotes:

[1] Friedrich Nietzsche, *The Will To Power*, Ed. Walter Kaufmann, (New York, New York: Vintage Books, 1967) p. 157.
[2] Ibid, p. 19.
[3] Ibid, p. 33.
[4] Ibid, pp. 461-462.
[5] Ibid, p. 159.
[6] Ibid, p. 156.
[7] Ibid, p. 159.
[8] Ibid, p. 40.
[9] Ibid, p. 41.
[10] Thomas Kuhn, *The Structure of Scientific Revolutions*, (Chicago: University of Chicago Press, 1970) p. 68.
[11] Ibid, pp. 92-93.
[12] Ibid, p. 93.
[13] Ibid, p. 93.
[14] Ibid, p. 93.
[15] Ibid, p. 93.
[16] Ibid, pp. 93-94.
[17] Ibid, p. 122.
[18] Ibid, p. 111.
[19] Ibid, p. 150.
[20] Friedrich Nietzsche, *The Will To Power*, Ed. Walter Kaufmann, (New York, New York: Vintage Books, 1967) p. 473.
[21] Karl Marx, *A Contribution To A Critique of Political Economy*, ed. Maurice Dobb, (Moscow, Russia: Progress Publishers, 1970) p. 21.
[22] Ibid, pp.20-21.
[23] Thomas Kuhn, *The Structure of Scientific Revolutions*, (Chicago: University of Chicago Press, 1970) p. 204.
[24] Ibid, p. 151.

Ch.7:

Sickness Unto Death & The Iron Cage Of Bourgeois-Capitalism

(The Case For Demolitionism)

According to Max Weber, the increasing rationalization and bureaucratization of civilization is the central problem for any industrialized society. In fact, the increasing rationalization and bureaucratization of everyday life across the globe is the key to understanding both the successes and the drawbacks of increasing, high-tech. industrialization. For Weber, everything comes down to maximum efficiency and, for Weber, bureaucratic rational organization is the epitome of achieving maximum efficiency. Underlying Weber's assessment of rationalization and modern bureaucracy, as a means of achieving maximum efficiency, is the notion of merit, namely, the notion that those individuals or entities, which maximize efficiency to the highest degree are those most apt to rise in any bureaucratic hierarchy. However, contrary to Weber, this is not the case. In fact, the opposite is the case.

In actuality, contrary to Weber, it is those individuals or entities which are most guided by irrationality, venal-cronyism, self-interest, and egoistical drama, which are most apt to rise in any bureaucratic hierarchy. The cream does not rise to the top, but instead, constantly lingers on the bottom, or upon, the lower and middle-echelons of any bureaucratic hierarchy. The reason for this is the fact that any bureaucratic hierarchy is first and foremost designed to reproduce a ruling set of ideational comprehensive frameworks, or ideologies, which underlie an institution's reason for being.

In contrast to Weber, there are no neutral bureaucracies or hierarchies in the sense that bureaucracies and hierarchies are in place foremost to reproduce meta-narratives, i.e., a ruling overarching mythology which governs and gives meaning to a specific civilization. And, in and across western high-tech. civilization, it is the Enlightenment meta-narrative of bourgeois-capitalism, which rules over all bureaucratic hierarchies. In effect, the meta-narrative of bourgeois-capitalism weaves a mythology that envelops bourgeois bureaucracies and capitalist hierarchies in an aura of legitimacy, progress and merit. Despite the fact, this mythology is a fiction, an arbitrary order and a falsity. It is not the most rational individuals or entities, which rise in modern bourgeois bureaucracies, it is religious fanatics, i.e., those individuals or entities which fuse their identities completely with the ruling meta-narrative of bourgeois-capitalism, which ascend into the upper-echelons of bourgeois-capitalism. It is those individuals or entities which are most guided by irrationality, venal-cronyism, self-interest, and egoistical drama, which are most apt to ascend the bureaucratic hierarchies of bourgeois-capitalism. Rationality has very little to do with career-advancement, despite what Weber says, pertaining to the increasing rationalization and bureaucratization of everyday life.

First and foremost, according to Weber, despite the many benefits which rationalization and industrialization produce, in and across industrial societies, there is also a slew of disadvantages that go along with this increasing rationalization process, specifically, rampant disenchantment, instrumentalism, and heavy bureaucratization. As Weber states,

> It is the destiny of our era, with its characteristic rationalization and intellectualization, [that]

> disenchantment [infects] the world, that precisely the ultimate and most sublime values have withdrawn from the public sphere [in the name of]...bureaucracy. [1]

For Weber, on the one hand, the socio-economic emphasis on rationalization produces many benefits in the way of efficiency, rational calculation, and the maximization of resources, in attaining specific social goals. However, on the other hand, there is a cost to this rationalization in the sense that this emphasis on the rational organization and bureaucratization of everyday life, means the fragmentation and disappearance of cultural values, including the loss of human identity and loss of human freedom, which is correct. Humans, under rampant rationalization and bureaucratization are plagued with a sickness unto death, i.e., despair.

Notwithstanding, Weber presumes that the most rational beings in a society are in control of bureaucracies, namely, bureaucratic hierarchies have an inherent process in them, designed to weed-out incompetence, stupidity, and collusionary-network-cronyism in the name of maximum efficiency, which is not true. The truth is in fact the opposite. In reality, rationalization and bureaucratization only serve to propagate, reproduce, and safeguard a ruling meta-narrative. Nothing else really matters. That is, rationalization and bureaucratization only serve to propagate, reproduce, and safeguard the meta-narrative of bourgeois-capitalism, including its best agents and fanatical proponents. Meaning, the primary reason for any bourgeois-capitalist hierarchy and bureaucracy is to perpetuate the meta-narrative of bourgeois-capitalism. Of course, this means that bourgeois-capitalist hierarchies and bureaucracies must at certain unavoidable times, and in certain unavoidable spaces, service the general-population, but, this is only a secondary objective. The prime directive for any bourgeois-capitalist bureaucracy and bourgeois-capitalist hierarchy is to maintain and perpetuate the meta-narrative of bourgeois-capitalism and, by default, the fanatical agents and venal-proponents of bourgeois-capitalism.

According to Weber, the essential motivation for human action in modern society and public affairs is no longer based on value-principles, understanding, and compassion for another, but instead, motivation for human action is increasingly based on the maximization of efficiency, performance and scientific quantification, etc. As Weber notes,

> rational calculation... reduces [everyone] to a cog in a [bureaucratic] machine. [And,] the passion for bureaucratization...drives us [increasingly] to despair. [2]

This is accurate, but, what Weber fails to mention is that this despair is the gateway to the true aim of bureaucratization and rationalization, that is, the establishment of a grand-mythology, a mythology designed to remedy modern industrial disenchantment and despair, if only an individual gives-in to the grand-mythology. It is in this manner by which the meta-narrative of bourgeois-capitalism batters down all alternatives and perpetuates itself, ad infinitum. Career-advancement is at your finger tips, if only you subscribe wholeheartedly to the meta-narrative of bourgeois-capitalism. All that is needed for ascension to the upper-echelons of bourgeois-capitalism is ideological congruity and zealous religious belief in the tenets of bourgeois-capitalism.

For Weber, the loss of value-principles, which were meant to guide industrial societies, increasingly led and leads to cultural fragmentation and cultural ossification, since, western civilization and western cultures become increasingly rutter-less and dependent upon instrumental rationality for any form of guidance. For Weber, the logical conclusion of rationalization and bureaucratization is that the general-population is increasingly condemned to an iron cage, an iron cage of bureaucracy and instrumental rationality, which is true. However, contrary to Weber, the loss of value-principles, which can guide industrial societies, is not specifically replaced by the neutral criterion of efficiency and maximum performativity. No, instead, the loss of value-principles is replaced by the meta-critierions of bourgeois-capitalism, that is, the maximum performativity of bourgeois-capitalism. As a result, this is a far more insidious form of rationalization and bureaucratization, than Weber ever conceived, since, it is a specific, myopic form of rationalization and bureaucratization, namely, bourgeois-capitalist rationalization and bureaucratization.

Building on Weber's notion of the iron cage, the iron cage is not just any old iron cage, neutral and un-bias. It is an iron cage specific to the meta-narrative of bourgeois-capitalism. It is the iron cage of bourgeois-capitalism. That is, an iron cage under-laid with a litany of arbitrary rules and bureaucratic procedures, designed solely to safeguard and perpetuate the meta-narrative of bourgeois-capitalism.

Indeed, in the end, for Weber, rationalization is de-humanizing and ultimately results in the enslavement and domination of humanity through evermore refined, hard-line, rational bureaucratic hierarchies and organizations. However, contrary to Weber, these refined, hard-line, rational bureaucratic hierarchies and organizations are not neutral, because, they reflect the meta-narrative of bourgeois-capitalism.

Of course, Weber is correct when he states that industrial societies welded to ever-increasing rationalization become bureaucratic machines, devoid of individuality and freedom. However, these bureaucratic machines are not necessarily hell-bent on maximum efficiency for efficiency's sake, as Weber argues. Despite the fact, rationalization replaces the amelioration of social ends with the amelioration of means without concise ends, in contrast to Weber, bureaucratization and rationalization always service a ruling meta-narrative, specifically, the ruling meta-narrative of bourgeois-capitalism.

Therefore, contradicting Weber's argument that the result of bureaucratization and rationalization is bureaucracy for bureaucracy's sake and rationalization for rationalization's sake, devoid of purpose and value-principles, the objective of our current form of bureaucratization and rationalization is not neutral or anything like what Weber suggests. In actuality, today, bureaucratization and rationalization is specifically bourgeois-capitalist bureaucratization and bourgeois-capitalist rationalization. If, according to Weber, "the world [becomes]... filled with [nothing but] little cogs, little men clinging to little jobs and striving for bigger ones"[3], these little cogs are increasingly clinging to capitalist-jobs and bourgeois hierarchies, striving for higher positions in and across the stratums of the bourgeois-capitalist-edifice.

In short, it is true, as Weber states, that the inherent process of rationalization structures the social affairs of industrial society in a bureaucratic fashion, wherein, there are highly-integrated networks of bureaucratic hierarchies and chains of command, efficiently, organized to maximize resources on a large societal scale, but, contrary to Weber, this is not a neutral rationalization process, it is a bourgeois-capitalist rationalization process, whose primary goal is the propagation and reproduction of the meta-narrative of bourgeois-capitalism.

For Weber, western capitalist countries need bureaucracy in order to function and operate efficiently, but, this criterion of efficiency is arbitrary and highly dubious in the sense that efficiency is measured and calculated on the basis of what organizational form, mechanism, and individuals, best serve the dictates of bourgeois-capitalism. The criterion of efficiency is the criterion of bourgeois-capitalist efficiency. As a result, the best and the brightest individuals, i.e., the most rational individuals, in and across western industrial societies, are increasingly being left-behind and/or left on the lower-rungs of the socio-economic ladder. The reason is because to be truly rational is to be unfettered by any meta-narrative, specifically, the meta-narrative of bourgeois-capitalism, and bourgeois-capitalism does not permit such a thing. Consequently, when the criterion of efficiency, career-advancement, and progress is determined by the narrow-confines and limited-parameters of the meta-narrative of bourgeois-capitalism, industrial societies suffer at the hands of bourgeois incompetence, capitalist stupidity, and the incessant ravages of bourgeois herd-mediocrity, which have risen far beyond their socio-economic value and competence. Under this overwhelming mediocrity in the upper-echelons of the bourgeois-capitalist-edifice, instrumental-rationality turns into an impediment to human development and progress. In effect, society ossifies into rampant inequality, socio-economic immobility, and retrogressive forms of rational bureaucratic organization and bourgeois-hierarchy. Society increasingly starts to collapse under the weight of its own overarching ineptitude.

All in all, rationalization and bureaucratization is supplanting value-principles, emotions, and sympathy in the name of efficiency, scientific quantification and instrumentalism, but because, rationalization and bureaucratization is subordinated to the meta-narrative of bourgeois-capitalism, it is supplanting them, contrary to Weber, with the criterion of bourgeois-efficiency, scientific capitalist quantification and bourgeois-capitalist instrumentalism. In effect, society and reason, subordinated to the meta-narrative of bourgeois-capitalism, destroy themselves, they kill their own reasonable pro-genies in favor of degenerate zeros, zeros that are elevated in the upper-echelons of the system in bull-shit jobs, wreaking havoc on the social fabric, due to the fact that their elevated positions are beyond their intellectual and emotional capacities.

In contrast to Weber, humans are not just becoming mere impersonal machines, as Weber believes, humans are becoming much more, they are becoming bourgeois-capitalist machines, programmed with specific bourgeois-capitalist rules and objectives. That is, the rules and objectives dictated to them by the meta-narrative of bourgeois-capitalism, which are furthermore imprinted onto the institutions and hierarchies of bourgeois-capitalism. In general, humans are not just being enslaved by bureaucratic machines and instrumental-rationality, impartially. Conditions are far worst. In the end, humans are becoming the bureaucratic slaves of specific bourgeois-capitalist machine-like institutions, that is, the myopic instrumental-rationality of bourgeois-capitalism. Wherein, humans now live, breath, and sacrifice their life-blood, freely of their own accord to the grand-mythology of bourgeois-capitalism, regardless of their own survival and happiness. They will do anything to stave-off sickness unto death, i.e., despair, the despair of extreme rationalization and bureaucratization. In consequence, as Weber states, they are being slowly and willingly transformed into "specialists without spirit, sensualists without heart; [wherein,] this [vast] nullity imagines that it has attained a level of civilization never before achieved"[4], but, in fact to the contrary, this nullity sinks evermore into the depths of misery, bureaucratic lunacy and deprivation, all in the name of bourgeois-capitalism.

All told, such progress is regress. Such freedom is slavery, when, rationality is taken to its ultimate extreme and its ultimate conclusion, that is, bourgeois-capitalism. The iron cage is no longer benign, as Weber argues, it is irrevocably malignant and cancerous. It is the meta-narrative of bourgeois-capitalism, at once a leap forward into the future and a step backwards into the morass of irrationality, venal-cronyism, self-interest, and egoistical drama at the expense of genuine rational intelligence, namely, intelligent poly-rationality. Therefore, the logical argument and case for demolitionism, that is, the total demolition of bourgeois-capitalism in the name of radical, egalitarian, post-modernity, i.e., post-modern anarchism.

Endnotes:

[1] Max Weber, *Science As A Vocation*, ed. H.H. Gerth and C. Wright Mills, (New York: Free Press, 1946) p. 155.

[2] Max Weber, *Economy And Society: An Outline of Interpretative Sociology*, ed. G. Roth and C. Wittich, (Berkeley: University of California Press, 1978) p. 41.

[3] Ibid, pp. 1000-1001.

[4] Max Weber, *The Protestant Ethic and the Spirit of Capitalism*, Trans. Talcott Parsons, (New York: Routledge, 1992) p. 124.

Ch.8:

Herd-Mediocrity & The Meta-Narrative of Bourgeois-Capitalism:

(The Case For Demolitionism)

The Enlightenment meta-narrative of bourgeois-capitalism is committed to mediocrity. In fact, the Enlightenment meta-narrative of bourgeois-capitalism celebrates it. Everywhere, the meta-narrative of bourgeois-capitalism reigns supreme, mediocrity follows, due to the fact, mediocrity is the order and the criterion of any type of hierarchy founded on the Enlightenment meta-narrative of bourgeois-capitalism. Indeed, as Nietzsche states, under such rubric "one and all [is] adjusted…to the most dubious mediocrity"[1], as the meta-narrative of bourgeois-capitalism concerns itself, foremost, with the propagation, the celebration, and the production of itself, i.e., bourgeois mediocrity, in and across, the stratums of everyday life and socio-economic existence. The point is profit. The reason is because mediocrity is most profitable and the most obdurate socio-economic substance any socio-economic formation, or narrative, can fashion for itself. Meaning, bourgeois mediocrity increases capitalist profit and the chances of duration, longevity, and resilience, pertaining to capitalist ruling power.

Bourgeois mediocrity is a congealed, unyielding, mass of citizens, intolerant to social change, novelty and liberty in the sense that bourgeois mediocrity wants its own suppression, enslavement, and homogenization, which the capitalist ruling power can readily accommodate, easily. Mediocrity is a herd, according to Nietzsche, it is a bulbous mass, stringently

> against [differences] of all kinds. [That is,] conservative…par excellence, slow to adopt, reluctant to let go, and [highly] enduring in the midst of … tremendous change and mixture of elements. Mediocrity [is]… consolidated and solidified [around a grounding] truth. [Its herd] is always mediocre and solid.[2]

In this regard, for Nietzsche, herd-mediocrity is "inertia… [where] the middle….is considered the highest and most valuable"[3] in the sense that this middle-of-the-road "herd mentality is forever directed towards stand still and [its] preservation"[4]. This is bourgeois mediocrity, par excellence. And, due to this fact, the Enlightenment meta-narrative of bourgeois-capitalism is dead-set on manufacturing, maintaining, and celebrating, bourgeois mediocrity of all types and kinds in its attempt to preserve and profit from its totalitarian supremacy.

Moreover, bourgeois mediocrity of all types and kinds is where capital accumulates in the greatest number, as bourgeois mediocrity is a dictatorial center, the average median and middle, which houses the greatest number of generic people, thus, the greatest sum of potential capital, i.e., surplus value. Bourgeois mediocrity is profitable. It is the most generic and the most average, therefore mediocrity, atop of being obdurate and unyielding to any type of change, is also the biggest reservoir of untapped capitalist profit. Hence, the increasing emphasis and focus, by bourgeois-state-capitalism, on averages, medians, and generic middles etc., that is, the dictatorship of the middle and the dictatorship of bourgeois mediocrity, since, this is where maximum profit resides. For example,

> in its effort to maximize profit and its supremacy, the logic of capitalism ever-increasingly propels itself towards the lowest common denominator, [in search of maximum profit], where capital, authority and legitimacy is most robust, concentrated and abundant, namely, where the majority resides. This means that all types of commodities are increasingly trite, pointless, disposable and/or identical. Whether, politically and/or economically, all commodities are increasingly purged of substance, rareness, spirit and/or individuality so as to mimic the average stereotypes of the median majority. [In effect], the lowest common denominator, located in the most basic average general median, is the most profitable, the most powerful and the most fixed position within the parameters of [bourgeois-state-capitalism].[5]

Consequently, bourgeois mediocrity is the most inflexible form and profitable form the general-population can be fashioned into. And, this is exactly what the meta-narrative of bourgeois-capitalism, which is imprinted upon all the stratums of everyday life, does and/or attempts to do, at all times and in all spaces, in and across of the capitalist-system.

In effect, the consolidation of bourgeois mediocrity increasingly tries to exterminate all forms of heterogeneity, autonomy, and equality, through maudlin, sappy, popular tastes and generic ways of life, which, in fanatic fashion hunt, trap, and asphyxiate, all that is truly different, novel, heterogeneous, plural and post-modern. The goal of the meta-narrative of bourgeois-capitalism is to produce, disseminate, and propagate, endless rounds, stops and starts, of fashionable bourgeois mediocrity, i.e., profitable mediocrity, which can again, stimulate ever-new rounds of profitable mediocrity, ad nauseam.

Profitability breeds profitability. Mediocrity breeds mediocrity. And, mediocrity can only see, believe, and understand, its own kind, namely, universal bourgeois mediocrity as "herd-[mediocrity] seeks [only] to preserve one type…itself"[6], and more importantly, it "hates those who detach themselves [from its center]…[and thus mediocrity] turns the hatred of the all…against them"[7]. Bourgeois mediocrity only celebrates its own kind in a sort of lame over-excessive jubilation, such is, what the meta-narrative of bourgeois-capitalism does, or attempts to do, through its omnipresent spectacle, which is showered onto the general-population. The point is to captivate and manufacture bourgeois herd-mediocrity long-enough in order to siphon capitalist profits out of this herd-mediocrity, all the while, placing these capitalist profits into the hands of a state-finance-corporate-aristocracy.

Consequently, the meta-narrative of bourgeois-capitalism "presents itself as something enormously positive, indisputable and inaccessible. It says nothing more than 'that which appears is good [and] that which is good, appears"[8]. This omnipresent positivity is then channelled into capitalist consumption, whereupon, commodities connected to the herd-majority, and a sense of belonging to this herd-majority, are designed to reflect this omnipresent positivity, which is manufactured, by the meta-narrative of bourgeois-capitalism, through its controlling media-outlets, star-personalities and its incessant, bourgeois-propaganda. This is the primary reason why the Enlightenment meta-narrative of bourgeois-capitalism has to be smashed, demolished, and fragmented, beyond recognition, since, the meta-narrative of bourgeois-capitalism, endlessly promotes mediocrity, ad nauseam, namely, a type of bourgeois-capitalist mediocrity, which ultimately, stifles innovation, creativity, plurality, heterogeneity and the blossoms of post-modernism. Namely, the progress, plurality, and diversity, stemming from all the independent micro-narratives interweaving the island-pockets of anarchist post-modernity, dotting the capitalist-system.

According to Nietzsche, meta-narratives lack verity and grounding truth, they are imposed onto the world so as to make sense of it; a meta-narrative "decides the character of appearance, [namely] reality"[9]. However, for Nietzsche, there is "no limit to ways in which the world can be interpreted"[10], because, as Nietzsche states,

> underneath it all…there is no grand unity…[all] is perspectival appearance, whose origin lies in us. To this extent…the denial of …a truthful world, [or] being, is…the only way of thinking.[11]

The reason for this is due to the fact, all meta-narratives lack universal validity in the sense that all meta-narratives are illusory manifestations of the will to power in its attempt to establish and impose its own despotic framework on the world.

According to Nietzsche, "it is our needs that interpret the world…[that is] our lust to rule"[12], which imposes meaning and sense onto the world. And, out of this will to power, meta-narratives, like the Enlightenment meta-narrative of bourgeois-capitalism, have encroached upon western civilizations in an authoritarian manner. They have been utilized to build despotic dominions, both conceptual and material, pertaining to how the general-population thinks and acts within society. Without meta-narratives, according to Nietzsche, an infinite

> plurality of perspectives [awaits]…[as] there are not facts, [or truths, to hold us]. Everything is in flux, incomprehensible, elusive [and a matter of] our

> opinion. What man finds in things is nothing but what he himself has imported into them… [via his or her] will to power. [13]

In effect, for Nietzsche, plurality, flux, in-commensurability, and partiality are the central elements of the underlying human condition. Meaning, humans can never possess a complete comprehension and mastery over reality, phenomena and/or situations. They understand only partially from the finite limits of their positional perspectives, which are forever fleeting, due to the inherent flux and existential anarchy embodied in existence. All that meta-narratives can do is impose a one-dimensional interpretation on events and phenomena, impeding plurality, heterogeneity, and the blossoms of anarchist post-modernism. However, meta-narratives are totalitarian points of views, which are, in essence, arbitrary, artificial, and are solely designed to monopolize interpretation, power and knowledge.

For Nietzsche, such overarching perspectives, like the Enlightenment meta-narrative of bourgeois-capitalism, are designed to cultivate converts, namely, a herd of followers. Meta-narratives, like bourgeois-capitalism, require converts, i.e., believers, in order to establish their despotic dominion over reality. As a result, these converts are forced to exercise a certain level of self-denial and deception, on others and themselves, in order to manifest the plausibility and effect of truth, pertaining to the illusory universal verities of the ruling meta-narrative, specifically, the meta-narrative of bourgeois-capitalism.

For Nietzsche, any "truth is…the consequence of an illusion"[14], derived from its particular perspective, i.e., narrative. And, believers must learn to deny their sense of disbelief and, instead, impose the "artificially built chimera"[15], both on themselves and others, which a meta-narrative fashions. In actuality, all meta-narratives are chimeras. That is, a perspective arbitrarily and artificially imposed and applied to the world and reality, which is inherently without universal verity, other than, the fact it is "a tool of power [exercised by] the will to power"[16].

Subsequently, the Enlightenment meta-narrative of bourgeois-capitalism is but an arbitrary/artificial conglomeration of wills to power. It is a conglomeration of wills to power forming one giant will to power, designed to despotically impose an arbitrary/artificial order on the variability of phenomena, reality and socio-economic existence, devoid of any verity, other than, the fact that it is a manner by which to accumulate and monopolize power in the hands of a select few.

Moreover, according to Nietzsche, "for every age and every new type of [society] …new truths…[new] delusions, …new values"[17] are enunciated, for which the general-population must learn to abide by and accept as timeless verities. It is in this regard that the meta-narrative of bourgeois-capitalism transforms the general-population into an obedient, docile, herd-mediocrity, reflecting its bogus verities and baseless beliefs. Initially,

> the program of [bourgeois-capitalist] Enlightenment…was the disenchantment of the world; the dissolution of myths and the substitution of knowledge for fancy. [Yet] knowledge, which is power, knows no obstacles [and has resulted] in the enslavement of men [and their] compliance with the world's rulers. [18]

As a result, the Enlightenment, through its meta-narrative of bourgeois-capitalism, cunningly continues to exercise totalitarian control and domination over mankind, which is forced to increasingly accept and internalize a false, one-dimensional, abbreviated world-view imposed upon it. Bourgeois herd-mediocrity is a product of this imposition and enslavement. Indeed, once established, according to Nietzsche,

> the herd…consolidates its mediocrity and always goes against everything new and exceptional. The power of the herd [and its] institutions,…[are meant to] grind the unique into uniformity and turn it into herd.[19]

Bourgeois herd-mediocrity is the essential substance and reason for the longevity of bourgeois-capitalism and its ever-accumulating profit. It provides the state-finance-corporate-aristocracy of bourgeois-capitalism, with a bottomless reservoir of available and exploitable, capitalist profits, while, simultaneously, providing the meta-narrative of bourgeois-capitalism with an endless procession of religious, capitalist converts, ready to sing its praises. It is in this regard that, according to Hokheimer and Adorno, "in service of the present age, [the] Enlightenment [has] become [the] wholesale deception of the masses"[20]. Through its cherished meta-narrative of bourgeois-capitalism, the Enlightenment turns

> the evolution of the machine…into…the machinery of domination…[wherefore] technical and social tendencies, [now] interwoven, converge in the total schematization of men.[21]

And, the end result is mediocrity, profitable mediocrity, the most treasured output the meta-narrative of bourgeois-capitalism can construct for its continued survival.

The meta-narrative of bourgeois-capitalism is a machine, an ideational comprehensive framework, both material and conceptual, where all questions, problems and/or situations have their black and white answers/interpretations, yes and no procedures, where, all social-ills have their easy-fix solutions and scapegoats. And, once ingrained and programmed into the general-population, the meta-narrative of bourgeois-capitalism wreaks havoc in and across the workforce/population, grinding it down into an ironclad herd uniformity, mentality, and mediocrity, which can only serve capitalist profitability and bourgeois-capitalist authority, all the while, leaving the workforce/population confused, dumbfounded, brainwashed and/or socially embittered.

Notwithstanding, the consolidated red-thread weaving this herd uniformity, mentality, and mediocrity, is the red-thread of the Enlightenment, that is, the meta-narrative of bourgeois-capitalism, whose underlying "prime directive is forever to maximize the accumulation and extraction of … capital, by any means necessary…as soon as possible"[22]. Consequently, bourgeois herd-mediocrity is the primary product of the red-thread of bourgeois-capitalism, not the other way around.

In fact, without the meta-narrative of bourgeois-capitalism, the herd becomes post-modern, plural, poly-rational, and fully heterogeneous, devoid of bourgeois sensibilities, tastes and/or any overarching bourgeois aristocracy. When, anarchist post-modernism reaches its Nth degree, anarchist post-modernism will as well reach the pinnacle of its development, i.e., maturity, equality, plurality and heterogeneity, which can only mean the total demolition of bourgeois-capitalism. Without the red-thread of bourgeois-capitalism, total insurrection, and the realization of full-fledged, anarchist post-modernism, pure, simple, and unadulterated, devoid of any overarching authority and/or unified logic, other than, the poly-rationality of multiplicity, plurality, heterogeneity, and pragmatic-egalitarianism. Thus, the case for demolition, demolitionism is the answer, the equitable solution to the despotic-tyranny of the meta-narrative of bourgeois-capitalism.

Endnotes:

[1] Friedrich Nietzsche, *Twilight Of The Idols*, Trans. R.J. Hollingdale (New York, New York: Penguin Books, 1990) p. 75.

[2] Friedrich Nietzsche, *The Will To Power*, Ed. Walter Kaufmann (NewYork, New York: Vintage Books, 1967) p. 461.

[3] Ibid, p. 159.

[4] Ibid, p. 162.

[5] Michel Luc Bellemare, *The Structural-Anarchism Manifesto*: (The Logic of Structural- Anarchism Versus The Logic of Capitalism), (Montréal: Blacksatin Publications Inc., 2016) p. 46. b).

[6] Friedrich Nietzsche, *The Will To Power*, Ed. Walter Kaufmann (New York, New York: Vintage Books, 1967) pp. 161-162.

[7] Ibid, p. 157.

[8] Guy Debord, *Society of the Spectacle*, (Detroit: Black and Red, 1983) p. 12.

[9] Friedrich Nietzsche, *The Will To Power*, Ed. Walter Kaufmann (New York, New York: Vintage Books, 1967) p. 149.

[10] Ibid, p. 326.

[11] Ibid, pp. 13-15.

[12] Ibid, pp. 267-269.

[13] Ibid, pp. 327-328.

[14] Ibid, p. 326.

[15] Ibid, p. 302.

[16] Ibid, p. 266-267.

[17] Ibid, pp. 461-462.

[18] Max Horkheimer and Theodor Adorno, *Dialectic of Enlightenment*, Trans. John Cumming (New York: Continuum, 2000) pp. 3-4.

[19] Friedrich Nietzsche, *The Will To Power*, Ed. Walter Kaufmann (New York, New York: Vintage Books, 1967) pp. 461-462.
[20] Max Horkheimer and Theodor Adorno, *Dialectic of Enlightenment*, Trans. John Cumming (New York: Continuum, 2000) p. 42.
[21] Ibid, p. 35.
[22] Michel Luc Bellemare, *The Structural-Anarchism Manifesto: (The Logic of Structural-Anarchism Versus The Logic of Capitalism)*, (Montréal: Blacksatin Publications Inc., 2016) p. 69. c).

Ch.9:

The Lie & The Fallacy Of The Meta-Narrative Of Bourgeois-Capitalism:

(The Case For Demolitionism)

The meta-narrative of bourgeois-capitalism is an artificial, i.e., man-made construct, designed solely to indoctrinate, subjugate, and dominate, the general-population in service of a state-financial-corporate-aristocracy, that is, a select few, who are its active material and ideological agents. All the empty-promises and fools-possibilities, the meta-narrative of bourgeois-capitalism has showered unto the workforce/population has, in all intent and purpose, come to naught. These empty-promises and fools-possibilities have only served to occupy the workforce/population, while, the agents of bourgeois-capitalism have robbed the workforce/population of its property, i.e., capital, both quantifiable and un-quantifiable. Consequently, although the Enlightenment has not been wholly vanquished to the dustbin of history, since, the Enlightenment meta-narrative of bourgeois-capitalism continues to stalk the planet, the Enlightenment must not be resurrected, by any means. It must not be re-animated, all-over again, so that it can enact its tyranny over humanity, all-over again. The way forward is to leave the past in the past, where it belongs. The way forward is towards the nth degree of heterogeneity, equality and autonomy, devoid of any overarching, meta-narrative, especially the cunning hydra, that is, the Enlightenment meta-narrative of bourgeois-capitalism.

In actuality, the meta-narrative of bourgeois-capitalism is, according to Max Stirner, nothing but "a spook…a fixed idea"[1], that is, "an idea that has subjected [people] to itself'[2]. It is a spook, and as a spook, the meta-narrative of bourgeois-capitalism imposes a certain manufactured feeling upon a person, pertaining to certain subject-matters and states of affairs. This feeling is not derived from the person, him or herself, it is not of his or her own volition, but, this feeling, or feelings, is derived from somewhere outside the person in the sense that it is imposed upon the person via certain, artificially, manufactured ideas, which are propagated by various social institutions, which reflect the meta-narrative of bourgeois-capitalism.

Subsequently, a person becomes possessed by the idea and/or the spook. He or she becomes a vehicle or medium of the fixed idea, which is ruling him or her. This is the illness, concerning the Enlightenment meta-narrative of bourgeois-capitalism. It is a spook, a set of phantasms, haunting the human head, whereupon, people move about, robotically, as if possessed by something other, which they certainly are. As Stirner states, these people "have wheels in [their] heads"[3], that is, an ideational comprehensive framework ruling over them, which, in effect, determines their thought-patterns and behaviors. They exist, think, and act, not of their own accord, but at the beck and call of some mysterious, overarching, fixed idea, which is, beyond their full understanding and consciousness. Such is the power of the meta-narrative of bourgeois-capitalism over the general-population.

This mysterious, overarching other, or others, according to Stirner, prescribe "what and how we are to feel and think"[4], concerning certain states of affairs and certain subject-matters, "and before the sacred [spooks], people lose all sense of power and all confidence"[5]. Spooks, such as bourgeois-capitalism, are ideational comprehensive frameworks, which organize phenomena for us, leading us to certain conclusions about things, people and events. An ideational comprehensive framework is a

> logical structure of concepts and relations, [both conceptual and material], that [has] …attained a certain level of supremacy in defining, describing, categorizing and manifesting [a certain specific] reality. [6]

Ideational comprehensive frameworks determine how we understand phenomena, people and/or situations, namely, they enable us to manifest meaning out of phenomena, people and events, which invariably, commands certain forms of actions. In effect, for Stirner,

> He [or she] who believes in a spook [like bourgeois-capitalism]… seeks behind the sensual world a super-sensual one; in short, [through the spook] they produce and believe [in] another world, and this other world [is] the product of their mind… for their senses grasp and know nothing of another…non-sensual world. [7]

And, this is what the meta-narrative of bourgeois-capitalism effectively promises, opulence, equality, freedom, democracy, i.e., a luxurious super-sensual world, for every soul at a future point in time, care of the capitalist mode of production, which, in fact, never comes to pass. In effect, these opulent daydreams remain forever on the distant horizon like the carrot on a stick, driving the workforce/population onward evermore into bondage, debt and misery.

The meta-narrative of bourgeois-capitalism bewitches the workforce/population to accept its station at the bottom of the economic pyramid. The meta-narrative of bourgeois-capitalism bewitches the workforce/population to accept the mechanism of wage-labor for the greatest number, since, the mechanism of wage-labor is the means by which the greatest number are forced to surrender their power and capital to those stationed at the top of the economic pyramid.

In effect, the capitalist-system of wage-labor is, in fact, a type of piecemeal slavery, due to the fact that members of the workforce/population have to sell themselves, i.e., their labor-power, on daily basis, rather than, at a one-time interval akin to the traditional slave-system, where, once sold, the slave is taken care of by his master, for his or her whole life, once, having been sold.

Subsequently, under capitalist wage-labor, the laborer must sell, him or herself, daily or weekly, and furthermore, must take care of his or her own daily subsistence and survival via the wage he or she received for his or her labor-power, regardless, if this wage is insufficient for his or her daily survival. The workforce/population sells itself on a daily basis to individual capitalists in order to receive the monetary means to purchase goods from other capitalists for their own subsistence and daily survival. As Marx states, "to be a productive worker [within wage-labor system] is …not a piece of luck, but a misfortune"[8]. Meaning, the workforce/population is increasingly degraded and impoverished, in various ways, by the Enlightenment meta-narrative of bourgeois-capitalism, which imposes the wage-system unto the workforce/population, by means of property and the false-promise of universal opulence for all, in relative equal measure, at a certain point in the future.

As Guy Debord states, in *The Society of the Spectacle*, with "this necessity [for]… boundless economic development, the satisfaction of primary human needs is replaced by an uninterrupted fabrication of pseudo-needs"[9], wherefore, the workforce/population has to endlessly produce and consume in order to live and, in the eyes of bourgeois-capitalism, lives only to the extent that it endlessly produces and consumes, according to the dictates of bourgeois-capitalism. As a result, this means the production and consumption of countless pseudo-commodities, which are only designed to satisfy a litany of countless, artificially fabricated, pseudo-needs.

Of course, for all its short-comings, the meta-narrative of bourgeois-capitalism lays blame for this on everything and everyone, which does not ascribe to its specific brand of capitalist religiosity. Meaning, that all systemic failures and economic crises, which arise in and across bourgeois-state-capitalism are ascribed to a lack of faith and lack of belief in the meta-narrative of bourgeois-capitalism.

Notwithstanding, in the end, responsibility for the ever-increasing nihilism, in and across everyday life, genuinely, lies with the meta-narrative of bourgeois-capitalism. Due to the fact, the meta-narrative of bourgeois-capitalism, invariably, sows the seeds of discontent, melancholia, and meaninglessness, wherever its despotic, twisted logic, penetrates the microscopic abodes of the workforce/population. As Guy Debord states,

> the economic system founded on isolation is a circular production of isolation…from the automobile to television, all goods selected by the spectacular [bourgeois-capitalist] system are also its weapons for a constant reinforcement of the conditions of isolation, …[namely], an abundance of dispossession. [10]

In fact, the spectacle, which is, for Debord, a metaphor for the meta-narrative of bourgeois-capitalism, "is what binds [citizens] together"[11] in the sense that "the spectacle [is foremost an] instrument of unification"[12]. It is "the material reconstruction of the religious illusion"[13], which unifies people only according to the necessities of the logic of capitalism, namely, the profit-imperative. Synonymous, the spectacle, the meta-narrative of bourgeois-capitalism, "is a pseudo-sacred entity…working for an ever-expanding [bourgeois-capitalist] market… and…the proletarianization of the world"[14]. In sum, the spectacle, i.e., the meta-narrative of bourgeois-capitalism, is "the existing order's uninterrupted discourse about itself, its laudatory monologue…in the epoch of its totalitarian arrangement of the conditions of existence"[15]. Everything is done and everything is said so as to maximize capitalist profitability, by any means necessary.

The meta-narrative of bourgeois-capitalism is the thread that stitches the patchwork of in-commensurable micro-narratives, together. It is "ideology par excellence… [it] is materially 'the expression of the separation and estrangement between man and man'"[16], both within commodities and across bourgeois-state-capitalism, in general. The meta-narrative of bourgeois-capitalism is that which unifies diversity under one umbrella and one socio-economic imperative, the imperative of maximum profit, by any means necessary. Meaning, the meta-narrative of bourgeois-capitalism "is the basis of...thought [in and across bourgeois] society. [It is] a deformed consciousness of realities, which sets in motion real deforming acts"[17] based upon illusory capitalist pretenses. For the meta-narrative of bourgeois-capitalism, only its "illusion…is sacred…[and] the highest degree of illusion comes to be the highest degree of sacredness"[18], wherein, even the meta-narrative of bourgeois-capitalism, specifically centralized in the illusion of money, becomes worthy of worship and religious fanaticism.

Ultimately, the meta-narrative of bourgeois-capitalism is the zeitgeist of the post-industrial, bourgeois epoch, it is “a Weltanschauung which has become actual. It is a world vision which has become objectified”[19]. The meta-narrative of bourgeois-capitalism infects the infinite plurality of micro-narratives, forcing them to conform to the dictates of bourgeois-capitalism, namely, the imperative of maximum profit, by any means necessary. As a result, the Enlightenment, through the meta-narrative of bourgeois-capitalism, persists in a zombie-like state, haunting the nooks and crannies of the globe and daily life, cloaked, solely, in the spectacle that is frenetic economic activity. Now, having abandoned its former meta-narratives of emancipation and the attainment of absolute knowledge, the Enlightenment, reduced to the meta-narrative of bourgeois-capitalism, pillages the world of wealth. And, like bourgeois-capitalism, the Enlightenment nowadays is “vampire-like, [in that it] lives only by sucking the living, and lives the more, the more…it sucks”[20], downgrading everything and everyone to “the shop-keeping spirit”[21], the spirit which radiates outwards from the meta-narrative of bourgeois-capitalism.

In effect, the meta-narrative of bourgeois-capitalism impedes the full-development of anarchist post-modernism, it deforms and tyrannizes over the global workforce/population, impeding all communal developments, which cannot be scientifically quantified and utilized to augment capitalist profits. The meta-narrative of bourgeois-capitalism is, in essence, retrogressive, with the only exception to the rule, being the field of machine-technology, wherein, it gives full, unencumbered, free-reign, devoid of any ethical dilemma, if such machine-technology augments profit. All other fields, art, politics, economics, philosophy etc., must completely conform to the bourgeois status quo, champion the bourgeois status quo, ad nauseam, or nothing at all. And, in the end, this means the total mediocrity of the world, the subjugation of art, politics, economics, philosophy etc., to the profit-imperative and ideological congruence with the meta-narrative of bourgeois-capitalism, i.e., the Enlightenment.

Subsequently, today this fact has virtually extinguished creativity, innovation, individuality, plurality, and humanity, whereupon, inhumanity, superficiality, and in-humaneness, have today disseminated their infectious disease in and across existence via the dictatorship of the singular, homogeneous, world view of bourgeois-capitalism. Absolutely, nothing is permitted to survive, if it does not wholeheartedly conform to the parameters of bourgeois-capitalism, nothing. Meaning, all must wholeheartedly ascribe to the lunacy that is the meta-narrative of bourgeois-capitalism, or be slowly exterminated, one long minute at a time, from the face of the earth, bored to death. In sum, the meta-narrative of bourgeois-capitalism is a dictatorship, a dictatorship imposed upon real plurality, diversity, and equality, wherein, the dominant "ideology…reflects economic coercion…[where the freedom to choose is always] …the freedom to choose [what is] always the same"[22].

According to Nietzsche, with the death of God, due to the arrival of modernity, a certain disenchantment has taken hold of western civilization, due to bourgeois-capitalism, which has invariably plunged humanity into an everlasting despair. This disenchantment and despair is nihilism. For Nietzsche, nihilism is increasing, due the fact that universal values and meta-narratives are today increasingly exposed for what they are, falsities, paper-tigers, concealing the meaninglessness and valueless-ness of things and systems of thinking. As Nietzsche states,

> The end of Christianity…which turns against the Christian God (the sense of truthfulness)…[stems] from [the fact that the idea that] God is truth [is now false,] all is false. Everything [now] lacks meaning…[and] all interpretations of the world are…false [and in]…error. [23]

Of course, Nietzsche hoped this growing nihilism would enable an Über-mensch to rise from the ashes of the total devaluation of all values in the sense that the "over-man [is] the goal"[24]. However, Nietzsche was at a lost to accurately describe the full extent of this nihilism, beyond a few broad abstract statements. Nietzsche never surmised that atop of God's grave would be stationed the meta-narrative of bourgeois-capitalism, the new saviour and light of humanity. That is, a new scarecrow, meant to fill the void left-over by God's death, which would inspire a global consumerist hysteria, prompting, western civilizations to kneel in prayer and worship before the magical properties of capital/money, with all the zeal and extremism, once reserved, only for religious icons and holy fanatics.

In fact, the end result of this capitalist fanaticism is a new form of totalitarianism, a bourgeois totalitarianism, the totalitarianism of the capitalist marketplace and the bourgeois lifestyle at any cost. This totalitarianism for the capitalist marketplace and the bourgeois lifestyle kills the human and the humane, wherever it reigns. It does this in the name of an underlying, unyielding homogeneity, which is ironically cloaked in the superficial garbs of a shallow, superficial heterogeneity. Subsequently, the unique, the genuine, the real, the human, and the humane, are today reduced to rumble so as to make way for endless digital superhighways, and shiny bourgeois commodities, radiating submissive, lukewarm artificiality, and bland counterfeits, in all directions. All of which, are passed off onto the general-population, by the institutional mechanisms of bourgeois-capitalism, as heroic, hip, revolutionary, emblems of techno-scientific progress. Namely, the epitome of bourgeois-meritocracy, which, as Stirner states, "is nothing…[but] a lie"[25]. That is, a hallowed falsehood, devoid of substance and lasting characteristics, other than, the meta-narrative of bourgeois-capitalism, which interlinks these in-commensurable islands and capitalist commodities into a singular composition at the expense of the workforce/population. Wherein, the workforce/population is gradually reduced into servitude and serfdom.

Indeed, as Horkheimer and Adorno state, in *Dialectic of Enlightenment*, bourgeois-capitalism, today, "so confines [the population], body and soul, that they fall helpless victims to what is offered [to it]. [In fact,] the deceived masses are today [so] captivated by the myth of [bourgeois-capitalist] success… [that] they insist on the very ideology which enslaves them."[26]. This is the power of the meta-narrative of bourgeois-capitalism in the sense that "bourgeois [capitalist] civilization is …[obsessed with] the constant necessity for the individual to obey the rules"[27], which has only meant the total homogenization of the general-population to its rule.

In effect, via its "dense network of modern means of communication, the world has become so unified, [by bourgeois-capitalism,] that [genuine] differences [have disappeared]"[28], beneath an artificial veneer of superficial, commercialized, bourgeois manufactured differences, both human or otherwise. That is,

> under the levelling pressure of late industrial society, …[we see] the universal reduction of all…to [a singular] one….[where] the anger against all that is

> different is...[now] inherent in the [bourgeois-capitalist] mentality, [which] permanently... deprives... the [logical] faculty of thought. [29]

As a result, the meta-narrative of bourgeois-capitalism, the cornerstone of the Enlightenment, manufactures an artificial world, which seemingly, portrays a litany of differences, opinions and points of views; but, only does so superficially in the sense that beneath all the bourgeois-capitalist, manufactured, synthetic-differences lies an ironclad formal logic, which reduces everyday life and all differences to one overarching imperative, the profit-imperative.

In effect, today, all of humanity must conform to the logical necessities dictated by the ideals of "*homo economicus*", as portrayed by the meta-narrative of bourgeois-capitalism, or risk re-education, or worst, terror, "as the application of this [meta-narrative], ...necessarily entails a certain level of terror, whether soft or hard,...[given that one must be] commensurable or [else] disappear"[30]. It is in this regard that the Enlightenment meta-narrative of bourgeois-capitalism "is...delusion [and]...insanity, where all the pores of consciousness are blocked [by terror, so that] the masses [may be]... kept in the state of total apathy [in order to] make them [susceptible to]... fantastic [commercial] exploits"[31].

Therefore, the way forward can only be through radical heterogeneity, radical plurality and radical equality, post-modern anarchist revolution. That is, real conceptual and physical acts of demolitionism so as to rid everyday life and socio-economic existence of all overarching, meta-narratives. Especially, the cunning hydra, that is, the Enlightenment meta-narrative of bourgeois-capitalism, due to the fact that it is inherently fascist and totalitarian.

Ultimately, anarchist post-modernism demands and commands insurrection. That is, a devastating wild fire of insurrectionism and demolitionism in service of real heterogeneity, real autonomy and real equality, i.e., pragmatic-egalitarianism, in all its shapes and forms. The point is to demolish the ironclad unity of bourgeois-capitalism, to smash it into a million pieces, in order to bring forth a federation/patchwork of micro-narratives so that all can have equal say and an equal part to play in decision-making-authority, in relative equal measure, devoid of all despotic capitalist meta-narratives and/or any permanent dominance hierarchy.

Endnotes:

[1] Max Stirner, *The Ego and His Own*, Trans. Steven T. Byington (New York, New York: Verso, 2014) p. 36.
[2] Ibid, p. 36.
[3] Ibid, p. 36.
[4] Ibid, p. 58.
[5] Ibid, p. 64.
[6] Michel Luc Bellemare, *The Structural-Anarchism Manifesto*: *(The Logic of Structural-Anarchism Versus The Logic of Capitalism)*, (Montréal: Blacksatin Publications Inc. 2016) p.1.i).
[7] Ibid, p. 63.
[8] Karl Marx, *Capital (Volume One)*, Trans. Ben Fowkes (London Eng.: Penguin, 1990) p. 644.
[9] Guy Debord, *Society of the Spectacle*, (Detroit: Black and Red, 1983) p. 51.
[10] Ibid, p. 28-31.
[11] Ibid, p. 29.
[12] Ibid, p. 3.
[13] Ibid, p. 20.
[14] Ibid, p. 25-26.
[15] Ibid, p. 24.
[16] Ibid, p. 215.
[17] Ibid, p. 212.
[18] Ludwig Feuerbach, *"Preface to the Second Edition of the Essence of Christianity", Ludwig Feuerbach: The Fiery Brook, Selected Writings*, Trans. Zawar Hanfi, (New York, New York:Verso, 2012) p. 258.
[19] Guy Debord, *Society of the Spectacle*, (Detroit: Black and Red, 1983) p. 5.
[20] Karl Marx, *Capital (Volume One)*, Trans. Ben Fowkes. (London Eng.: Penguin, 1990) p. 342.

[21] Max Stirner, *The Ego and His Own*, Trans. Steven T. Byington (New York, New York: Verso, 2014) p. 95.
[22] Max Horkheimer and Theodor Adorno, *Dialectic of Enlightenment*, Trans. John Cumming (New York: Continuum, 2000) pp. 166-167.
[23] Friedrich Nietzsche, *The Will To Power*, Ed. Walter Kaufmann (New York, New York: Vintage Books, 1967) p.7.
[24] Ibid, p. 519.
[25] Max Stirner, *The Ego and His Own*, Trans. Steven T. Byington (New York, New York: Verso, 2014) p. 20.
[26] Max Horkheimer and Theodor Adorno, *Dialectic of Enlightenment*, Trans. John Cumming (New York: Continuum, 2000) pp. 133-134.
[27] Ibid, p. 198.
[28] Ibid, p. 204.
[29] Ibid, pp. 206-208.
[30] Jean-Francois Lyotard, *The Post-Modern Condition*, Trans. Geoff Bennington and Brian Massumi (Minneapolis: University of Minnesota Press, 1984) p. xxiv.
[31] Max Horkheimer and Theodor Adorno, *Dialectic of Enlightenment*, Trans. John Cumming (New York: Continuum, 2000) pp. 204-205.

Ch.10:

The Post-Modern Anarchist Revolution

I

Because, post-modernism does not go far enough, because post-modernism has not reach the zenith and apex of its critique and programme, due to the fact, it has been divorced from its motor force, anarchism, revolution/insurrection is unavoidable. In fact, post-modernism demands it, it demands the total realization of anarchism, that is, its own essence. Post-modernism demands the full-maturation of its inherent principles, radical equality, radical plurality and the total demolition of all meta-narratives. Its only recourse is post-modern anarchist revolution.

In contrast, the meta-narrative of bourgeois-capitalism impedes post-modern growth and post-modern development, at every turn. And, bourgeois-capitalism refuses to secede its rule and its dominion to intelligence and the future, calmly and quietly. As a result, revolution is unavoidable and a must. The revolution is a post-modern anarchist revolution. Namely, a revolution organized to overthrow all the lasting meta-narratives of the Enlightenment, specifically, bourgeois-capitalism. The objective of the post-modern anarchist revolution is nothing less than radical plurality, radical equality, and radical pragmatic-egalitarianism in all its shapes and forms.

Nothing must be left unchanged. The post-modern anarchist revolution shall reach its logical conclusion, only when anarchist demolitionism rids the earth of the Enlightenment meta-narrative of bourgeois-capitalism, including the state-finance-corporate-aristocracy built and sustained upon it.

Paraphrasing Karl Marx that "the capitalist mode of production…begets, with the inexorability of a natural process, its own negation, [wherefore]…the development of …industry…cuts from under its feet [its] very foundation"[1], according to Nikolai Bukharin, revolutions emanate from the antagonism between the forces of production and the relations of production, inside the dominant mode of production of an epoch. As Bukharin states,

> the cause of revolution, of a violent transition from one type [of society] to another, must be sought in a conflict proceeding between the productive forces, and their growth, on the one hand, and…the production relations on the other hand. [2]

In essence, it is the radical disconnect between the productive forces of a society and its production relations, inside a dominant mode of production, which, if not rectified, eventually results in the violent overthrow of society, that is, the violent overthrow of the current, dominant, socio-economic framework of a society.

Specifically, according to both Marx and Bukharin, this is exactly what happened with the rise of bourgeois-capitalism and the capitalist mode of production on the back of the feudal mode of production. However, whereas, Bukharin argues that revolutions are due to the productive forces having outgrown the envelope of production relations, for post-modern anarchism, it is the other way around. It is the networks of production relations which outgrow the productive forces and, in effect, begin to press heavily upon the productive forces so as to make them evolve, or perish.

New relations of production require new organizational forms of production, i.e., new configurations of productive forces. In essence, new networks of relations embody new sets of requirements. And, this demand for new requirements places undue pressure upon the forces of production. They must meet these new requirements through reorganization or perish.

For Bukharin and Marx, "the evolution of the production relations is conditioned by the movement of the productive forces"[3], while, for post-modern anarchism, it is vice versa. It is the evolution of the productive forces that is conditioned by the movement of the relations of production. Namely, demand determines supply, consumption determines production. Therefore, contrary to Bukharin and Marx, it is the new requirements of the relations of production which stimulate the technological evolution of the productive forces. And, when the productive forces cannot evolve to accommodate the new parameters and expansions of the relations of production, revolution, catastrophe, and crisis, ensues in order to re-configure the sum of the productive forces along a new set of relations, a new mode of production. It is relations which inevitably drag the forces of production into the future.

Indeed, in a rare slip, Bukharin acknowledges the supremacy of socio-economic relations over the productive forces when he states, "it is upon the production relations of cooperation [and equality], maturing in the womb of capitalist production relations, in general, that the temple of the future will rest"[4]. Meaning, it is the relations of production, not the productive forces, which is the bedrock for any revolutionary change.

Contrary to Bukharin, according to post-modern anarchism, productive forces only buttress socio-economic relations, they do not determine their form and content. The productive forces mirror and reflect the relations of production, it is the relations of production which constantly bring forth new forces of production so as to maintain and perpetuate, themselves, not the other way around as Marx and Bukharin would have us believe. As a result, revolutions stem from the active side of the antagonism between the forces of production and the relations of production, inside a dominant mode of production. In short, it is the living and dynamic relations of production that instigate revolution, not the dead and static productive forces of capital.

Contradicting his own notion of the supremacy of the productive forces over the relations of production, Bukharin even states "revolutions [always] begin… with ideology [and end with] technical revolutions, a sort of reverse order, as it were."[5], where, in the final analysis, relations of production are deemed superior to the productive forces in the sense that it is always the relations of production which lead the way into the future. Therefore, according to post-modern anarchism, it is the dynamic socio-economic relationships, which interweave the social fabric and exert command over the forces of production, which instigate revolution, not the forces of production. The revolution of the relations of production precede the revolution of the forces of production, not vice versa.

Revolutions begin in and across the relations of production and end with the re-arrangement and transformation of the forces of production, which are violently re-configured, or transformed, anew to service the newly, established networks of productive relations, which have arisen prior, during, and after the revolution.

And, whenever, conceptual and material acts of demolitionism transpire, in large numbers, in and across everyday life, socio-economic relations have developed new needs and new requirements. And, these new needs and requirements are pressing evermore upon the old organizational forms of the productive forces. In effect, the forces of production and their organizational forms have remained stagnant and, because of this, increasing acts of demolition have ensued. As a result, for post-modern anarchism, technological revolutions are founded on new relations of production, that is, socio-economic relations, demanding more evolved productive forces, which better align with the new requirements of these newly-minted relations. In short, technological revolutions do not precede new relations of production, they develop and grow out of them so as to accommodate the new set of relational requirements. Demolitionism is a consequence of this conflict and these crises.

Following Bukharin's notion that the initial step towards revolution "takes place when…objective evolution places the oppressed…in an intolerable situation…causing [the oppressed] to feel clearly that no improvement can be obtained under the existing order"[6], a gestalt-switch is needed. In turn, post-modern anarchism stipulates that revolutions begin with disillusionment and nihilism, i.e., radical shifts in the relations of production, rather than, radical shifts in the forces of production. As Bakunin states, the people "are made revolutionary by necessity, by the intolerable realities of their lives, their violent hatreds…[being] illegitimately diverted to support…the exploiters of labor,…the bourgeoisie"[7]. Consequently, for post-modern anarchism, akin to Bukharin, it is intolerable situations, whatever these may be, arising from the networks of productive relations, which stimulate revolutionary change and acts of demolition.

Contrary to Bukharin, Marx and the communists, it is not the evolution of the productive forces which drive societies towards revolution, it is the evolution of the relations of production. It is outmoded and obsolete forces of production, which are made outmoded and obsolete by the arrival of new relations, new ways of connecting, arising out of the bustling daily-interactions of people, which drive societies towards revolution. It is not the forces of production. The reason is that productive forces are inanimate, passive and, in the end, their evolution is guided by the relations of production; while, in contrast, the relations of production are animate and active, constantly bustling and buzzing with frenetic activity. It is the frenetic networks of relations which inadvertently prompt abrupt leaps and brakes with the old organizational framework of productive relations and forces of production. This is what sparks revolutions, demolitions and radical social change.

Indeed, from the perspective of post-modern anarchism, the initial catalyst to revolution is radical social change in the old networks of socio-economic relations, prompting radical change in the old networks of productive relations, which in turn, themselves, increasingly come to weigh heavily upon the old forces of production. The old mode of production either re-organizes itself and/or succumbs to bolder and bolder acts of demolitionism.

If the old forces of production are able to evolve and meet the new requirements of the newly, re-configured, socio-economic relations, then, crisis is rectified and averted. If not, the new requirements of the newly, re-configured, socio-economic relations smash the old organizational form of the forces of production into irreparable pieces, resulting in systemic breakdown, revolution, demolition, and eventually, the re-configuration of society upon a new foundation, that is, a new mode of production. Namely, a new mode of production that is more conducive to the new burgeoning networks of socio-economic relations, i.e., the new relations which have thrown-off the old production relations, including their old organizational form.

In short, all evolutionary and revolutionary capacities lie within the evolutionary and revolutionary capabilities inherent in the networks of socio-economic relations. The litany of competitive dynamic interactions within the networks of socio-economic relations, either spearheads technological revolution and the continued stability of the meta-narrative of bourgeois-capitalism; or instead, result in the demolition of the meta-narrative of bourgeois-capitalism and the foundation upon which this meta-narrative is welded and bonded. If the bourgeois-capitalist mode of production is a vertical, centralized, homogeneous mode of production, which it is, then, in all likelihood, the post-modern, anarchist mode of production is, or shall be, a horizontal, decentralized, heterogeneous mode of production, that is, a set of multiple modes of production centred around autonomy, equality and heterogeneity, rather than, bourgeois-capitalist unity, inequality and uniformity, namely, any omnipresent bourgeois herd-mediocrity.

II

According to Bukharin, over an extended period of time, it is inevitable that "production relations [become such an] emphatic…brake on the evolution of the productive forces that [both productive forces and production relations] simply must be broken up if society is to continue to develop"[8]. And, if the productive forces, including the relations that direct these productive forces, are not burst asunder in order to accommodate the newly-minted socio-economic relations, then, according to Bukharin, "the entire society will become stagnant and retrogressive, i.e., it will enter upon a period of decay" [9]. Such is the case with the

Enlightenment meta-narrative of bourgeois-capitalism and the bourgeois-capitalist system, it is stagnant and retrogressive in nature and, thus, must be demolished and burst asunder as bourgeois herd-mediocrity reigns supreme, along with a degenerate, state-finance-corporate-aristocracy.

Essentially, the entire contemporary capitalist edifice and the bourgeois socio-economic landscape have descended into a stagnant, retrogressive period of decay, because, the old socio-economic relations of bourgeois-capitalism, best exemplified in the ruling oligarchy, cling fanatically to the outmoded capitalist-mode of production. They cling to a set of socio-economic relations which in fact hinder socio-economic development, stifling growth and the advent of the post-modern/anarchist age.

Indeed, an outmoded capitalist-mode of production, bent on continuing, ad infinitum, invariably kills-off anything, or anyone, which threatens its rule, even, if this means killing off any possibility of socio-economic growth and/or development. Specifically, the senile capitalist mode of production and its antiquated, state-finance-corporate-aristocracy, are resolved to stifle all new sets of burgeoning relations of production, which might be antithetical to the meta-narrative of bourgeois-capitalism and its own existence.

Therefore, today, the objective of bourgeois-capitalism is to maintain the trajectory of socio-economic retrogression and decay, by any means necessary, since, the outdated capitalist mode of production supports a small antiquated elite, whose survival is welded to the failing capitalist mode of production. In short, the senile capitalist mode of production supports a specific set of organizational relations over another subset of organizational relations, which threaten its rule. Consequently, the proponents of the outdated capitalist mode of production, i.e., the state-finance-corporate-aristocracy, deny with certain religious-fanaticism, the basic fact that western societies have entered into a period of terminal, socio-economic retrogression and decay.

In fact, the reality of this retrogression and decay is emphatically denied and passed-over in silence by the ruling institutions of the ruling relations of production. In contrast, such socio-economic retrogression and decay is passed-off onto the general-population as a form of socio-economic progress and development via elitist propagandist machines. That is, the empty-celebratory monologue of bourgeois-capitalism, droning on and on, ad nauseam, celebrating bourgeois-centrism as the most reasonable and the most revolutionary. In effect, today, the monologue of bourgeois-capitalism drones on and on throughout the capitalist mass media, about the glorious superiority of bourgeois-capitalism over all other forms of organization. Wherefore, to be reasonable is to be bourgeois and to be bourgeois is to be part of the capitalist vanguard, a dependable stern proponent of the meta-narrative of bourgeois-capitalism.

Notwithstanding, according to Mikhail Bakunin, revolutions are a natural fact, they occur regardless of any controlled preparations undertaken by the ruling powers that reign over capitalist society. Indeed, states Bakunin,

> revolutions [are] a natural fact…[they do] not take place according to a preconceived plan but [are] produced by uncontrollable circumstances, which no individual, [or group] can [predict or] command. [10]

Therefore, similar to Marx's claim that "crises can only be educed from…capitalist production, competition and credit"[11] and, in the final analysis, are truly unpredictable, for Bakunin, revolutions are as well an inescapable fact of the capitalist mode of production and bourgeois-capitalism, in general.

For, both Bakunin and Marx, "capital contains within itself the possibilities of [endless] interruptions"[12], interruptions, which are in essence unpredictable, random, and at times explosive. Consequently, a post-modern anarchist revolution is a revolution founded upon "local and spontaneous organization" [13], an organization, which mirrors and reflects the seeming spontaneity and randomness of economic crisis. The post-modern anarchist revolution is in essence incessant interruption, without end or solution, culminating in the demolition of the meta-narrative of bourgeois-capitalism, namely, a total gestalt-switch and paradigm-shift.

Like Bakunin's notion of revolution, the post-modern anarchist revolution, is a revolution sparked by an intolerable situation, requiring nothing less than a total gestalt-switch and paradigm-shift, requesting,

> freedom for all individuals as well as collective bodies, associations, communes, provinces, regions. [Such a revolution]...seeks the confirmation of... equality [for all] by [establishing] economic equality [for all]. [Of course,] this is not the removal of natural differences, but equality in the social rights of every individual from birth... [to] equal means of subsistence, support, education...and equal resources and [access to] facilities [for all]. [14]

Therefore, the objective of any post-modern anarchist insurrection is to do away with all meta-narratives, specifically, the meta-narrative of bourgeois-capitalism, while, establishing a series of anti-capitalist and post-capitalist institutions, which emphasize maximum equality, autonomy and heterogeneity. As a result, to quote Bakunin, the post-modern anarchist revolution starts by

> destroying, above all, all…[bourgeois-capitalist] institutions and…[bourgeois-capitalist relationship] organizations [like] churches, parliaments, tribunals, administrations, banks, universities, etc., which constitute the lifeblood of the [bourgeois-capitalist] state. [The bourgeois-capitalist] state must be entirely demolished and declared bankrupt…[so] the people in the…[anarchist] communes [may collectively] confiscate…all state property [for themselves]. [15]

To have a successful post-modern anarchist revolution, it is necessary to pragmatically demolish, both conceptually and materially, bourgeois-capitalist socio-economic conditions, i.e., capitalist forces of production and capitalist relations of production, in order to install a patchwork plurality of autonomous-collectives, narratives and worker-cooperatives.

Specifically, a successful post-modern anarchist revolution will demolish the concept of private property and the bourgeois-state so as to foster forms of communal organization that maximize equality, autonomy and heterogeneity. To quote Bakunin, the goal is to have a society where all micro-narratives have equal access to resources, in relative equal measure, whereupon, no-one is privileged over anyone else and "workers take possession of all [forms of] capital and the tools of production" [16], whether, these are conceptual tools and/or material tools. No meta-narrative must be allowed to have dominion over the plethora of micro-narratives, sharing the sum of capital, in relative equal measure.

In brief, the post-modern anarchist "revolution requires extensive and widespread destruction, a fecund and renovating destruction, since, in this way and only this way are new worlds, [relations and productive forces] born"[17]. The ultimate goal of any post-modern anarchist "revolution is the extirpation of the principle of [totalitarian] authority"[18]. That is, it is the eradication and demolition of all despotic, overarching meta-narratives, specifically, the meta-narrative of bourgeois-capitalism in favor of a horizontal-constellation of microscopic narratives, sharing the sum of socio-economic resources, equally. Namely, a horizontal-constellation of micro-narratives which exercise decision-making-authority, among themselves, with relative equal force, devoid of any centralized, hierarchical, state-apparatus or meta-narrative.

In sum, any post-modern anarchist revolution, including any post-modern, anarchist, socio-economic formation, is a type of heterogeneous formation exercising power "from all points. [Whereupon, power does] not depend on a single directing center. [In effect,] the center [is] not... the source, but the product [of the periphery.] [It is] not the cause, but, the effect"[19] of the peripheral, horizontal-constellation of micro-narratives. This set of peripheral micro-narratives, determining the political-economic center, are to be organized in a manner by which they can freely express their localized authority, together, onto one another, in relative equal measure, where none is superior to another. The result is an equilibrium of force and power between a varying array of horizontally organized micro-narratives. These micro-narratives are to function and operate, together, as a loose shifting federation or collective-patchwork, devoid of any overarching meta-narratives, specifically, the meta-narrative of bourgeois-capitalism. They are to function and operate as an open-participatory-democracy.

All told, the post-modern anarchist revolution is perpetual. It is permanent. It is the demolition of meta-narratives, bourgeois-capitalism, without end. The post-modern anarchist revolution shall reach its end, only when, the earth trembles from end to end with the awesome power of demolitionism, radical post-modern anarchism!

Endnotes:

[1] Karl Marx, *Capital (Volume One)*, Trans. Ben Fowkes, (London Eng.: Penguin, 1990) pp. 929-930.
[2] Nikolai Bukharin, *Historical Materialism: (A System of Sociology)*, (New York, New York: International Publishers, Martino Publishing, 1925) p. 244.
[3] Ibid, p. 244.
[4] Ibid, p. 253.
[5] Ibid, p. 262.
[6] Ibid, p. 256.
[7] Mikhail Bakunin, *Bakunin On Anarchy*, ed. Sam Dolgoff, (New York: Vintage Books, 1972) pp. 191-192.
[8] Nikolai Bukharin, *Historical Materialism: (A System of Sociology)*, (New York, New York: International Publishers, Martino Publishing, 1925) p. 249.
[9] Ibid, p. 249.
[10] Mikhail Bakunin, *Bakunin On Anarchy*, ed. Sam Dolgoff, (New York: Vintage Books, 1972) p. 357.
[11] Karl Marx, *"Crisis Theory", The Marx-Engels Reader*, ed. Robert C. Tucker (New York, New York: W.W. Norton & Company, Inc., 1978) p. 455.
[12] Ibid, p. 464.
[13] Mikhail Bakunin, *Bakunin On Anarchy*, ed. Sam Dolgoff, (New York: Vintage Books, 1972) p. 180.
[14] Ibid, pp. 96-97.
[15] Ibid, p. 100.
[16] Ibid, p. 358.
[17] Ibid, p. 334.
[18] Ibid, p. 202.
[19] Ibid, p. 180.

Conclusion:

If anything, this series of essays should convince readers as to the validity of anarchism working within post-modernism and vice versa, including, the verity that the advent of post-modernism has not reached its full-maturity as of yet, since, post-modernism is only now aware of its engine, anarchism. The fact is the full-brunt of post-modernism has been impeded by the last remaining meta-narrative of the Enlightenment, i.e., bourgeois-capitalism, due to the fact that post-modernism until now has been divorced from its motor force, anarchism. Consequently, the myths of bourgeois-capitalism have cunningly continued to dominate the sum of socio-economic existence. Specifically, the bourgeois-capitalist myth that promises socio-economic opulence and luxury-comforts for all, if people just ascribe and follow to the letter the fundamental imperative of bourgeois-capitalism, the maximization of capitalist profit, by any means necessary, as soon as possible.

The point of the Enlightenment meta-narrative of bourgeois-capitalism is to deny cooperation, collectivism, pluralism and any form of pragmatic-egalitarianism. The point is to encourage radical individualism, social Darwinism, dependence and bourgeois-hierarchy as the essential verities for a good life, and for the advancement of the human species as a whole. The meta-narrative of bourgeois-capitalism is fundamentally reactionary and antithetical to progress, if this progress does not coincide with the myopic imperative of bourgeois-capitalism, profit-making. As a result, the meta-narrative of bourgeois-capitalism is gradually driving humanity into inhumanity, order into chaos, and society into social-Darwinist barbarism, wherein, might is right, all of the time, and social mobility is ossified into a feudal, bourgeois-capitalist pyramid.

The only option out of bourgeois barbarism is radical anarchism. Anarchism fused with post-modernism, insofar as the objective of post-modern anarchism is the overthrow of the meta-narrative of bourgeois-capitalism, in all its forms, while, replacing bourgeois-capitalism in return with an anarchist federation/patchwork of micro-narratives. Wherein, each is equally given an equal amount of decision-making-authority, absent of any hierarchy founded on the tenets of bourgeois-capitalism. The apex of post-modern anarchism is maximum equality, namely, equality founded on economic financial equality for all. As a result, for both post-modernism and anarchism, equality starts with economic financial equality. There cannot be equality among people, unless, there is first and foremost economic financial equality among people. Consequently, the apex and full-maturity of post-modernism has not yet occurred. It is still on its way, due to the fact that only now is post-modernism getting reacquainted with the revolutionary force of its powerful engine, anarchism. Ultimately, this revolutionary force is driving towards total equality, total autonomy, and total heterogeneity, devoid of bourgeois-capitalism and/or any totalitarian meta-narratives.

Any post-modern anarchist revolution has this as its goal, namely, open-participatory-democracy, devoid of socio-economic inequalities and meta-narratives. In fact, any post-modern anarchist revolution is designed to reinvests the general-population with decision-making-authority. That is, the decision-making-authority which was taken from the general-population, decades ago, by the agents and proponents of bourgeois-capitalism. Therefore, the objective of the post-modern anarchist revolution is to do away with meta-narratives, all-together, so as to liberate the plethora of micro-narratives, suffocating beneath the military boot of bourgeois-capitalism.

In brief, this text is a call to arms for the abolition of all meta-narratives, including the state-finance-corporate-aristocracy. It is a call for the abolition of all forms of bourgeois-sycophantism, venal cronyism, and degenerate opportunism, which incessantly station private property over and above collective prosperity. Finally, only by pushing the tenets of post-modernism and anarchism to their ultimate conclusions will civilization and societies open themselves up to creative possibilities and scientific opportunities, where a fully-automated, post-modern, luxury anarchism is truly possible, devoid of all forms of bourgeois-capitalist racketeering. In the end, the choice is yours, but, the choice is nothing less than post-modern anarchist revolution. As, this is a bomb, nicely packed in a brown paper bag, left outside the revolving-doors of the bourgeois-capitalist edifice, eloquently, exposing that this so-called grand-narrative is but another absolute metaphysical nothing, ready to die.

"Anarchism, Now! Anarchism, Forever! Anarchism, The Future!"
MLB/2018

Bibliography:

Bakunin, Mikhail. *Bakunin On Anarchy*. ed. Sam Dolgoff. New York:Vintage Books, 1972.

Bellemare, Michel Luc. *The Structural-Anarchism Manifesto: (The Logic of Structural-Anarchism Versus The Logic of Capitalism)*. Montréal: Blacksatin Publications Inc., 2016.

Bellemare, Michel Luc. *Treatise On Nihilism*. Montréal: Blacksatin Publications Inc., 2017.

Bukharin, Nikolai. *Historical Materialism: (A System of Sociology)*. New York, New York: International Publishers, Martino Publishing, 1925.

Debord, Guy. *Society of the Spectacle*. Detroit: Black and Red, 1983.

Derrida, Jacques. *A Derrida Reader: Between The Blinds*. ed. Peggy Kamuf. New York: Columbia University Press, 1991.

Derrida, Jacques. *Of Grammatology*. Trans. Gayatri Spivak. Baltimore: Johns Hopkins University Press, 2016.

Feuerbach, Ludwig. *"Preface to the Second Edition of the Essence of Christianity". Ludwig Feuerbach: The Fiery Brook, Selected Writings*. Trans. Zawar Hanfi. New York, New York: Verso, 2012.

Feyerabend, Paul. *Against Method.* London: Verso, 1975.

Foucault, Michel. *Society Must Be Defended*. Trans. David Macey. New York: Picador, 1997.

Foucault, Michel. *The Archeology of Knowledge*. Trans. A.M. Sheridan-Smith. New York, New York: Routledge, 1972.

Foucault, Michel. *The History of Sexuality*. Trans. Robert Hurley. New York, New York: Vintage Books, 1990.

Harvey, David. *The Enigma of Capital*. Oxford, United-Kingdom: Oxford University Press, 2010.

Horkheimer, Max and Theodor Adorno. *Dialectic of Enlightenment*. Trans. John Cumming New York: Continuum, 2000.

Kuhn, Thomas. *The Structure of Scientific Revolutions*. Chicago: University of Chicago Press, 1970.

Lyotard, Jean-Francois and Jean-Loup Thebaud. *Just Gaming*. Trans. Wlad Godzich. Minneapolis: University of Minnesota Press, 1985.

Lyotard, Jean-Francois. *The Differend: Phrases in Dispute*. Trans. Georges Van Den Abbeele. Minneapolis: University of Minnesota Press, 1988.

Lyotard, Jean-Francois. *The Post-Modern Condition*. Trans. Geoff Bennington and Brian Massimo. Minneapolis: University of Minnesota Press, 1984.

Malatesta, Errico. *Errico Malatesta: His Life and Ideas*. ed. Vernon Richards. London: Freedom Press, 1984.

Malatesta, Errico. *The Method of Freedom*. ed. David Turcato. Edinburgh, Scotland: AK Press, 2014.

Marx, Karl. *A Contribution To A Critique of Political Economy*. ed. Maurice Dobb. Moscow, Russia: Progress Publishers, 1970.

Marx, Karl. *Capital (Volume One)*. Trans. Ben Fowkes. London Eng.: Penguin, 1990.

Marx, Karl. *"Crisis Theory,". The Marx-Engels Reader*. ed. Robert C. Tucker. New York, New York: W.W. Norton & Company, Inc., 1978.

Marx, Karl. *"Economic and Philosophic Manuscripts of 1844". The Marx-Engels Reader*. ed. Robert C. Tucker. New York, New York: W.W. Norton & Company Inc., 1978.

Marx, Karl. *"Grundrisse", The Marx-Engels Reader*. ed. Robert C. Tucker. New York, New York: W.W. Norton & Company, Inc., 1978.

Marx, Karl. *"Manifesto of the Communist Party". The Marx-Engels Reader*. Ed. Robert C. Tucker. New York, New York: W.W. Norton & Company Inc., 1978.

Marx, Karl. *"Theses on Feuerbach", The Marx-Engels Reader*. ed. Robert C. Tucker. New York, New York: W.W. Norton & Company, Inc., 1978.

Nietzsche, Friedrich. *Twilight Of The Idols*. Trans. R.J. Hollingdale. New York, New York: Penguin Books, 1990.

Nietzsche, Friedrich. *The Will To Power*. Ed. Walter Kaufmann. New York, New York: Vintage Books, 1967.

Proudhon, Joseph. *What Is Property?*. United-States: Loki's Publishing, 2017.

Schumpeter, Joseph A. *Can Capitalism Survive? (Creative Destruction And The Future of The Global Economy)*. New York, New York: Harper & Row, 1950.

Srnicek, Nick and Alex Williams. *Inventing The Future: Post-Capitalism And a World Without Work*. New York: Verso, 2015.

Stirner, Max. *The Ego and His Own*, Trans. Steven T. Byington. New York, New York: Verso, 2014.

Weber, Max. *Economy And Society: An Outline of Interpretative Sociology.* ed. G. Roth and C. Wittich. Berkeley: University of California Press, 1978.

Weber, Max. *Science As A Vocation.* ed. H.H. Gerth and C. Wright Mills. New York: Free Press, 1946.

Weber, Max. *The Protestant Ethic and the Spirit of Capitalism.* Trans. Talcott Parsons. New York: Routledge, 1992.

Wittgenstein, Ludwig. *Philosophical Investigations.* Trans. G.E.M. Anscombe. New Jersey: Prentice Hall, 1958.